D0882781

CROP CIRCLES

CROP CIRCLES

Signs, Wonders and Mysteries

STEVE AND KAREN ALEXANDER

CHARTWELL BOOKS, INC.

THIS BOOK IS DEDICATED, WITH LOVE AND APPRECIATION, TO OUR FAMILIES: HAZEL AND ALEC, NITA AND JOHN, DEBBIE AND GEOFF, VIVIEN AND JOHN AND ESPECIALLY TO OUR DAUGHTER, KAYLEIGH

This edition printed in 2008 by

CHARTWELL BOOKS, INC.
A Division of **BOOK SALES, INC.**
114 Northfield Avenue
Edison, New Jersey 08837

ISBN-13: 978-0-7858-2069-7
ISBN-10: 0-7858-2069-8

Printed in China

Contents

BEGINNER'S MIND

In Zen philosophy, they speak of something called 'Beginner's Mind'. It is where we attempt to go back to the beginning of something; a state of 'focused openness' where our preconceptions, and everything we think we already know about something, are temporarily set aside. It is often used when we feel we have reached a plateau of thought or come up against a brick wall and need to look at something anew. It is to become (for a while) timeless in our thinking, to unburden ourselves of our fixedness, our presumptions, even our prejudices, in the hope of finding fresh perspective or insight.

The subject of crop circles is difficult to raise in polite company these days without the obligatory joke about it all being a hoax. All the beauty, poetry and grace that they exhibit simply pass many people by, unnoticed, unrealized – an unreality. It seems that the subject has become something of a cultural embarrassment, especially to the English, who still can't quite believe that they once fell for an obvious confidence trick by two men who wanted to fool the world into thinking that ET was talking to us. For the embarrassed, the crop circles remain to this day hermetically sealed behind a wall of rejection, not to be examined lest anyone be fooled again.

But, while many have walled themselves off from crop circles, the circles themselves have quietly and consistently continued to appear. In fact, since the heady days of 1990 and the height of their fame, they have progressively become more and more sophisticated and complex. Around fifty to sixty circles appear each summer in the UK alone (sometimes significantly more), with many more occurring worldwide – most notably in Germany, the Netherlands, Norway and Italy, as well as the USA and Canada; all regularly report the phenomena during their summer months.

Crop circles vary in size, from a few feet across to over a thousand feet in either diameter or length. In the UK, the average diameter is about 200 feet, hardly an insignificant size. These incredible works of geometric art are no small undertaking; nothing about them is casual, slapdash or unintelligent, quite the contrary, their designs are often incredibly clever and inventive – some even border on the realm of genius itself.

On design alone, the crop circles of the past fifteen years or so deserve a second look, as so much of what they symbolize is intelligent, significant and even pertinent to our world. The crop patterns might even be considered, on some level, powerfully transformative and instructive.

This book is about those designs and what they embody, the meaning that lies beneath the shapes and the perennial knowledge they seem to employ. It is about their variety and diversity and, paradoxically, their unity of language and ultimately their universality. A foray into the world of the crop circles can be edifying and even enlightening. It is a journey worth making the time to take.

But, how might we begin to break this cultural taboo, shake off enough of the baggage the crop circles can bring with them and begin to separate the wheat from the chaff? Perhaps we need to find that state of focused openness that Zen calls Beginner's Mind.

EVERYTHING AND NOTHING

SCIENCE AND HOAXING

From their very inception, the crop circles have steadfastly resisted our attempts to fit them into our current world-view. They have tantalized but so far eluded science and despite the claims of hoaxers and rationalists, they have refused to be completely explained away as an elaborate deception. At present, crop circles remain one of the most stubborn challenges to our view of what constitutes our reality because although they are there for us to experience, they do not fit in comfortably with our understanding of the world.

The public profile of the circles appears cyclical, seeming to rise and fall in waves. Every now and again, there will be a crop circle of such complexity or magnitude that it will tweak the public interest, but for every peak there is a corresponding trough, as new hoaxers and detractors come along to counter any resurgence of interest.

For all the hostility, it has to be said that the crop circles do not seem to care about what is said about them. They have continued their revelations undisturbed and undeterred throughout the years. Even in 2001, when much of the farm land in the UK was declared off limits due to the outbreak of foot and mouth disease, they continued to appear as usual. Government restrictions may have placed them out of reach to ground researchers, but they could still be recorded photographically from the air – seen and understood, their forms drawn and contemplated.

The vast majority of circles appear fully formed overnight, in the space of six or seven hours (sometimes less) during the summer months. Most are picture-perfect with no mistakes, even though formations are often hundreds of feet in diameter and created in the dark. If crop is flattened manually, there is no lifting it up again to cover a mistake.

Crop circles, it seems, have a life and agenda of their own and there is something about the doggedness of their persistence that, if nothing else, deserves our respectful attention. It is as if these giant expressions are borne of some imperative; a need to convey or illustrate something vitally important. This apparent compulsion becomes simultaneously more eloquent and more profound with each passing season.

To date, the work of biophysicist William Levengood forms the most comprehensive and credible scientific study of the subject. He has a background in research for the agricultural seed industry and so is well placed to investigate what might be happening. Levengood has detected some unusual characteristics in connection with both the soil and crops of the circles. He has found definite, demonstrable changes, which he insists are not accountable for by hoaxing alone. These changes occur at molecular and cellular levels and include specific changes to the nodal points of wheat and barley stems, which are seen to bend or rupture from the inside outwards. Whilst Levengood does not go as far as to speculate on the ultimate origin of such changes, he does believe that microwave energy may be involved, which superheats the crops for a fraction of a second, affecting the moisture content and causing the plants to soften and fall over, cooling in a horizontal position. This superheating also accounts for the nodal rupturing (these are called 'expulsion cavities') and the general bending of the nodes – the parts of the plants that store moisture. Furthermore, testing shows that this heat energy (as evidenced by the varying extents of changes observed in the sampled plants) conforms to known patterns of energy distribution, such as Beers Law. The soil samples collected also show unusual changes. Crystalline formations and even microscopic nodules (or 'spherules') of meteoritic iron, have been found and photographed – perhaps suggestive of a strange atmospheric effect at work. A number of papers by

Levengood have appeared in peer-reviewed scientific journals that deal specifically with plant physiology, indicating that his work is well-regarded and has some independent scientific credibility.

The crop circles seem to teeter precariously between scientific fact on the one hand and the realm of the hoax-artists on the other. Although two or three of them might be faked for the press each year, the vast majority of circles go unclaimed. It is interesting (and rather depressing) that in the fifteen or so years since the first hoax was reported, the media have never tired of wheeling out the same well-worn story every summer. Such stunts claim by inference that the whole phenomenon is a joke – a claim that ignores the science. I have often wondered if the hoax theorists have fully considered the science, or have simply discounted it because, for them, it can't be true.

A stalemate has been reached between the assertions made by scientific investigation and the idea that all circles are a hoax. Neither one can wholly account for the phenomenon; neither one can claim to have the argument entirely sewn up. This leaves the crop circles occupying a strange position, in which their origins cannot be wholly proved or disproved.

THE THIRD PLACE

A CHANGE IN EMPHASIS AND PERCEPTION

Geometrically and symbolically, the crop circles make a great deal of sense to many people. They appear to speak in a universal language of metaphor, allegory and myth; their patterns are full of significance and meaning that is hard to ignore. Taken as a body of work, these gigantic symbols and mandalas seem to express something very deep about the nature of the world, and suggest a means of looking at reality in an entirely new way.

Such has been the nature of the perpetual search for the circles' validation, that these less tangible elements have been largely ignored. We live in a world that finds worth only in those things that one can prove to be real; if there is no proof we tend to discount or dismiss things. The occurrence of crop circles has made this approach rather difficult, so with no end to the science–hoax stalemate in sight, we either choose to suspend all further work indefinitely or we have to transcend the argument altogether.

The interesting thing is that when you do loosen the tether on this dyadic state of affairs, you find that the symbolism and geometry of the circles is, in fact, a third way of probing their nature. No obstacle is put in your way, save the limits of your own imagination; the crop patterns are open-ended statements which you are free to explore at will.

Once this change in emphasis is engaged (from 'who' and 'how', to 'what' do they mean) the circles suddenly and magically unfold before your eyes. If it was not so bizarre, one might be forgiven for thinking that this is exactly what they want us to look at – not how they are made, or by whom – but what they might be saying.

After over fifteen years of following the crop circles closely, investigating and experiencing hundreds of them in person, I can honestly say that I do not know who makes them all or how – and I don't even know exactly why. But what I can tell you is that I have come to believe through their symbolism, geometry and metaphor that the crop circles represent or make visible some of the oldest and deepest questions man has ever asked. They appear as mirrors; pictures of our state of mind or of our aspirations, dreams and even, at times, our doubts and fears. To gaze at the circles is to gaze upon the mystery of mankind.

From the beginning, crop circles have presented us with shape, geometry and number: it is their very essence. Take, for instance, the circle (the shape that first appeared in the crops): it has no beginning or end; it encompasses more interior space than any other shape; and its circumference is unknowable as it cannot be accurately measured, which is why we have to use 'pi' (π) in order to approximate it. The mysterious and solitary nature of the circle has made it synonymous with divinity down the ages. It is loaded with symbolism, signifying a meaning beyond its functional form. It embodies a whole set of philosophical notions that can be derived from its properties; the 'qualities' of the circle.

The unfolding of number and order (shape) tells us

something fundamental about our reality. It reveals how matter is ordered by creation and, more than that, it tells us that this process is as meaningful as it is functional. The crop circles have consistently presented us with patterns that not only illustrate this process but also offer a commentary upon it.

These are not new ideas. Major civilizations have all, to a certain degree, been aware of and utilized such concepts. Plato's Utopia, the philosophy of Pythagoras and even St John's vision of the Kingdom of Heaven all embraced the same notions; these concepts have inspired and motivated man for thousands of years.

With the development of modern science, our perception of the world and ourselves changed. Science rendered such ideas unnecessary for the comprehension of our reality. However, the innate meaning of number and form is neither arbitrary nor superstitious; it is derived from the very nature of those numbers and shapes.

Number and form lie at the foundation of everything. They are the ordering principle behind the way matter is structured, from the tiniest particles to man himself. These shapes may even form the structure of one of the most mysterious creations in the known universe: consciousness.

Crop circles are challenging our grasp of reality as well as our current notions about the nature of life and creation. They seem to be re-tuning our perception, re-balancing the issues of function and meaning.

Once seen, the innate meaning imbued in the structure of all things does change one's view of reality. It breathes life into what seems lifeless and it gives meaning beyond purpose. The crop circles have changed the lives of many; they have started a silent revolution in thinking, one that 'en-souls' the world rather than rendering it a living machine or computer program.

Crop circles not only speak of elemental shapes and numbers but they also present themes and illustrate the archetypal principles that underpin them. Labyrinths, mazes, knots, ropes, tethers, spirals, all become part of a symbolic language that lies at the heart of the human psyche.

Those who perceive these things embodied in the crop circles and subsequently become aware of them in the wider world, will never see eye to eye again with those who do not. For those who only regard them as a prank or scientific curiosity, the circles do not tally with their reality constructs. Each side now inhabits a different reality; one side lives in the rational, logical and literal world, whilst the other lives in a reality in every way the same but deepened by symbol, metaphor and intrinsic meaning.

LANDSCAPE

STONE CIRCLES, EARTHEN MOUNDS AND FAIRY RINGS

It does not matter in which country the crop circles appear, they have a definite affinity with ancient sites. As you look through this book, you will notice the recurrence of many of the UK's famous henges and barrows. In the US, circles have appeared around Serpent Mound, a site sacred to the Native American tribespeople. Continental Europe also has many large megalithic (meaning 'big stones') sites in France, Germany and beyond.

Dowsers find the crop circles of particular interest; they detect all kinds of 'dowsable' energies in and around them. Sometimes the circles occur on ley lines (straight lines of energy that connect features of the landscape), which dowsers say criss-cross the whole earth; occasionally they happen at the centre of a group of old churches or above underground water systems. One piece of modern research showed that the circles favour underground aquifers and chalk. Those who investigate 'earth energies' speculate that underground water and chalk may emit some kind of piezoelectrical energy, which can generate strange atmospheric lights and may be connected to the appearance of the crop circles.

In the UK, there are many myths and legends that surround prehistoric sites. However, we are also beginning

Stonehenge

(RIGHT)

Stonehenge is the world's most famous stone circle. Surprisingly, it is not particularly large in area but the upright sarsen stones enclosing the central space are enormous (up to 22 feet in height). What distinguishes the design of Stonehenge from that of Avebury is the way huge lintels are used to connect the upright stones. Stonehenge is said to date back to 3100 BC, but recent discoveries suggest it may be much older.

Avebury Stone Circle

(LEFT BELOW)

There are two stone circles at Avebury, both enclosed within one larger one, which also has a huge stone avenue leading into the south side. Over the last thousand years, most of Avebury's stones were torn down for use as building materials in the village that now stands inside the circle. The stones were originally brought from the Marlborough Downs, where sarsens are to be found scattered in the wake of an ancient glacier. The sarsens used to build the centre of Stonehenge are from the very same place. Avebury dates from around 2500 BC.

Silbury Hill

(RIGHT)

Silbury Hill, near Avebury, is the largest neolithic mound in Europe (130 feet) and is thought to have been built in three stages, starting about 2660 BC. Under the earthen cover, there is a six-stepped conical structure built in alternate layers of earth and chalk. It was probably a vast communal undertaking that created the ceremonial centre. Silbury Hill has been likened to the breast or the pregnant belly of the Earth Goddess; it also has been described as an 'Orgone Accumulator' – a device for the collection of natural earth energies.

to realize how sophisticated our ancient ancestors were; their use of geometry and measure in the creation of stone circles and barrows is far more advanced than first thought. It is obvious that many of the sites are connected to astronomy. Understanding the heavens was very important to early man. Not only was it useful to be able to predict the changing seasons, there is much evidence to suggest that the ancients also took an interest in the movement of the sun, moon and stars, and especially rare, celestial events such as eclipses of the sun and the moon.

In the UK, the huge stone circle complex at Avebury in Wiltshire is a focus for crop circles; almost every year they appear in the fields surrounding the site. Avebury is the largest stone circle on the planet – many times larger than Stonehenge. Whilst Stonehenge has seen many crop circles over the years and its stones are bigger than those at Avebury, it is Avebury that attracts more crop circles. Stonehenge was undoubtedly an astronomical observatory, its stones mark the cycles of the sun and the moon and could be used to predict eclipses. Avebury, on the other hand, is connected only to lunar cycles, linking it to the Neolithic cult of the Earth Goddess – who was also associated with the moon.

Ancient locations throughout the world are steeped in myth and folklore. The UK sites are often reported to be haunted not only by ghosts but also by earth spirits, pixies and fairies; the ancient god Pan is also a regular visitor. There are many stories of those who have come into contact with the Small Folk, dancing in fairy rings around barrows and stones. Before the days of alien abductions, people were frequently reported to have been carried off by fairies and spirits.

Any visit to a quiet, isolated barrow or standing stone can be an eerie experience. In many myths and legends these monuments are described as places where the veil between this world and that of the spirits has worn thin, providing a gateway for spirits to cross over into our realm.

LUMINOSITIES

THE POSSIBILITY OF OTHER REALITIES

During the summer of 1990, Steve Alexander travelled to Wiltshire in order to visit and film the crop circles. From the top of Milk Hill he looked down into the fields below and began filming a circle to the left of his vantage point. He had finished and was about to leave when suddenly a small flash of light drew his attention. It was travelling through the air from left to right in his field of vision; picking up his camera, he started to record its progress. The luminosity appeared as a small point or sphere of light and it moved from the direction of the crop circle he had been filming towards another, which was obscured from view by the bottom of the hill. The light passed over the wheat as it neared Steve's position, it then paused before dropping into the crop and moving around; it caused no disturbance in the standing wheat at all. For a short while, it ceased moving and Steve stopped the camera. However, it eventually resurfaced and went off with increasing speed across the field, away from the camera. Once more, Steve set about filming the event. The light then passed over the roof of a tractor that was turning a field; the tractor was seen to stop for a short time before resuming its task. Finally, the light travelled on and up towards the summit of Rybury Camp, an ancient hillfort in the distance. The camera attempted to follow the light up into the air but it was lost to the viewfinder. Throughout the duration of the film, Steve and his companion can be heard discussing possible explanations for what they are witnessing. They suggest a balloon, a bird, or a piece of paper, but neither seems convinced that they have hit upon the answer.

Steve's footage was the first to show this form of luminosity and its possible connection with the crop circles. Since that time, and with the growing number of video/camcorders available on the market, there have been more such recordings; sequences showing what appear to be small, brilliant white lights flying in proximity to the circles. When the tractor driver in Steve's film was traced, he described the light as being the size of a beach-ball, glinting and flashing. The driver was at a loss to explain why his tractor had stopped; the engine had simply cut out briefly before spontaneously restarting.

The most striking property of these luminosities is the nearer they come to the camera the smaller they get, whilst the further away they travel the larger they seem. Eye witnesses report that the lights are roughly spherical and range from the size of a tennis ball to that of a small beach-ball. In another sequence, the object is almost stationary but it flares several times before making a rapid arcing (or looping) manoeuvre into the crop. The brilliance

of the object dazzles the eye like burning magnesium but the crop remains unharmed. The motion is fascinating and can be attributed entirely to the light, since the camera was mounted on a tripod. In yet another sequence, the lights are seen to travel over a circle, just above the heads of visitors, before increasing to an incredible speed and disappearing into the distance.

When Steve Alexander's film footage was submitted for analysis in Japan, the technicians concluded that the object had no discernible dimension, and that in some frames the object was clearly present whereas in other frames it simply disappeared. They ruled out a conventional explanation for the light, such as a bird, insect or balloon, and said the object appeared to fade in and out of reality.

These lights seem to appear and disappear at will, but where do they appear from and disappear to? It is a question that UFO researchers have been asking for years. But I wonder if the Japanese researchers were closer to the truth than they imagined when they suggested that the ball of light seemed to fade in and out of reality.

So much about the crop circles seems aimed at challenging our view of reality; even the geometry of some formations can be seen focusing upon the convergence of two states of existence. Throughout this book, we will encounter crop circle shapes that employ such concepts as the Golden Section and the squaring of the circle; both of which symbolically address the bordering of realms. The squaring of the circle is representative of the meeting of heaven and earth or that of the spiritual and the physical, whereas the Golden Section speaks of the meeting between matter and the animating force that instigates growth, development and life – to many this is also a meeting of substance and spirit.

The scientific work carried out on the circles may also be suggestive of such and idea. The effects to the crop and soil seem to be almost alchemical in nature. The effects of circles upon the crop and soil seem to be almost alchemical in nature. Scientific analysis can reveal that crops have been affected but is at a loss to explain exactly how it came about. This parallels scientific analysis of alchemical matter. It is interesting to observe that alchemists insist some of the changes to their chosen elements occur as a result of the consciousness of the alchemist himself – another example of the meeting of matter and spirit.

A challenge to our accepted view of reality seems instilled in the crop circles at every level. It is an infinitely iterated concept which doggedly insists that we reconsider the bounds of what we currently call reality.

CHAPTER ONE

SACRED GEOMETRY AND NUMBER

PAINTING BY NUMBERS

It would be stating the obvious to say that in order to understand something about the crop circles we have to look at their geometry and number. The essence of the crop circles is their shape, measure, pattern and proportion – it is their very structure and language.

However, to enter this world is not just to learn something about the shapes of the circles; an inadvertent but fortuitous by-product is that we also begin to learn something about the underlying patterns of life, nature and the universe beyond. The geometry of the crop circles seems to express timeless, universal constants and elements found throughout the natural world, in everything from the tiniest flower to vast star-filled galaxies, and even in the design of our own human bodies. Number is often referred to as the 'universal language' and can be understood by anyone who can count.

Geometry means 'measure of the earth', and its practice is hoary with age. The need to quantify or measure area is an essential part of human culture; the demarcations of property and land boundaries are the first acts in the creation of any society. Man has observed for thousands of years the shapes, patterns and proportions which underlie the design of the natural world. The geometry of a tree or a flower is as demonstrable today as it was long ago, as are the ratios and proportions of the human body and its growth processes; geometry, it could be argued, is the world's oldest science.

However, to the Ancients, geometry and number were more than quantities and scientific functions; they embodied a canon of number, form and proportion that was used to build the whole of creation. These numbers, forms and proportions were therefore divinely inspired, the building blocks and apparatus of a divine creator. The Ancients took these principles and wove them into the fabric of their societies; they used them in their temples and precincts and reproduced the same divine order in their own sanctuaries and metropolises. In his theory of The Forms, Plato wrote about an archetypal canon of number, shape and proportion upon which creation was founded. These 'forms' existed in a perfect state beyond the physical world and were known to us only by inference – or via pure reason.

Another legendary Greek, Pythagoras, founded a whole philosophy of numbers based not just upon their quantities and forms, but also on the archetypal qualities that numbers can be seen to embody. Pythagoras was almost certainly not the first to associate numbers with these kinds of qualities, but it is from him that most of our modern understanding of such matters originates. The study of sacred geometry follows a symbolic creation myth, which uses geometric forms to describe the unfolding of order in space. Included in this myth are not only the numeric and geometric properties of numbers, but also their inherent meanings and functions (the second property of number). Once the basic vocabulary of this geometrical and numerical language has been grasped, it opens the door to a whole new realm of understanding shapes and patterns.

Shapes, patterns and proportions also play an integral role in the human psyche; it has been suggested that we are predisposed to see underlying patterns in all things. Certainly it has been shown that shapes, spaces and designs can have a profound unconscious effect on the mind – we may even have some kind of 'intelligence of shape and harmony'. Just as with Rorschach ink blots used in psychological profiling, we have an ability to detect order and form in the seemingly haphazard. It is this skill in part which helps us make sense of the things we see, sense and feel. Perhaps we feel a special empathy with certain archetypal shapes, because we are designed using the same

Cherhill, Wiltshire, England. July 1999. Wheat crop, approximately 200 feet

principles and somewhere deep inside us we sense this. Through psychology, we have become ever more aware of our patterns of behaviour and even our relationships can be likened to proportions and ratios – we often give them a form of measure by saying that some are closer and some are more distant.

Crop circle designs are often about economy, efficiency and expediency. Like the best designs in nature, the measures and proportions are often self-contained, and whilst seemingly multifaceted and beautiful, they employ the most ingenious and simple solutions for achieving the desired outcome. The patterns often use self-similarity, mirroring and regeneration at varying scales, and other such principles found in nature's design book. Themes develop over a season or more, beginning with simple forms which are then developed through several formations and brought to a conclusion. This is a fascinating part of the crop circle mystery, and one which allows us to follow the thought-processes of the mysterious circle-makers.

Once seen, these patterns, or universal truths, cannot be unseen: once we know something, we cannot then decide to 'unknow' it. Perhaps that is what the crop circles are intended for. Perhaps this also goes some way towards helping us understand why the crop circles can have such a life-changing effect: once seen, the geometrical aspect of the crop circles can change the way people perceive reality forever.

The following chapter will take you through the numbers one to thirteen and look at their properties, symbolic meanings and the crop circles that have utilized and expressed them.

ONE: UNITY AND ETERNITY

MONAD – THE CIRCLE

There is no other shape more pleasing than that of the circle, a continuous curve around a single point. A circle has no beginning and no end; it is the only shape that can be drawn in a single movement, a single sweep of the pencil around a compass point. It represents the eternal, wholeness, unity and perfection. For sacred geometers the circle represents the Divine, all that is, the one potentiality from which all else emanates.

'God is a circle whose centre is everywhere and whose perimeter is nowhere' – so said Voltaire using the circle as a metaphor for the omnipresence of God's being. God is often shown as a geometer in many classical paintings, illustrating that many artists have considered geometry a sacred science, whereby they followed in the footsteps of God by also using this sacred canon of number in their own creations – a canon of shape and proportion that permeates both the Earth and the Heavens.

Another unique and mysterious property of the circle is that, unlike any other geometrical shape, the sum of its perimeter is unknowable (who knows the true measure of the Divine?). We therefore approximate the perimeter (or circumference) of a circle by using the equation Circumference $=2 \pi r$, where r is the radius. Pi (π) is a mathematical device called an 'irrational number', used to create the illusion of an equilibrium of numerical values; in other words, it is used to approximate a number that is inexpressible in whole units. Pi = 3.142; a number whose decimal places would stretch into infinity, never finding a

Morgan's Hill, Wiltshire, England. August 2003. Wheat crop, approximately 80 feet

Avebury Henge, Wiltshire, England. August 1998. Wheat crop, approximately 300 feet

resolution. So, for our convenience, it is shortened to just three decimal places, ensuring a satisfactory solution to estimating the circumference of any given circle.

In his theory of The Forms, Plato postulated that when we draw a shape we may only ever approximate a universal form, one that exists in a state of perfection beyond our physical realm. That archetypal shape exists, like the Divine, in a state of flawlessness that we can only ever aspire to. In the case of the circle, this is quite true; we can all imagine a perfect circle, but in this physical reality we may never truly replicate it, or ever know its true measure. In rendering a circle as faithfully as we are able, we take part in a sacred act which pays homage to the perfection of the Divine.

AVEBURY HENGE, 1998

The simple ring at Avebury had a notable curiosity – it seemed to have further geometries implied in the laid crop. Several arch-shapes can clearly be seen, but appear to serve no practical function.

EXPRESSIONS OF ONE-NESS

The simple circle is the ultimate expression of one-ness. The very term 'crop circle' is derived from the fact that the phenomenon began as single, simple circles appearing in crop fields. One-ness is also expressed as an encompassing ring, sets of rings, or as a single, solitary formation. Often, more complex geometries are contained within an enclosing circle or outer ring, and this can provide a vital clue to hidden proportions beyond those overtly expressed by the pattern. Inside these formations, the laid crop often indicates a centre of swirl different from the geometric centre of the circle, although why this happens is unknown.

COLLINGBOURNE KINGSTON, 2005

The lovely set of concentric rings appeared in the stunning blue-purple of a borage field. The harmony of measure between the standing and flattened areas is quite beautiful. Borage is used in the production of several medicines, and this was the first time a circle had appeared in this type of crop.

THE RIDGEWAY, 2005

The magnificent Ridgeway rings (opposite) – nearly two hundred feet across – illustrated that simple is not always boring. To be inside this formation was like standing on the top of a huge vinyl record – walking around the circle, following the direction of the laid crop, I had the eerie feeling that I was the needle traversing the grooves, and found myself wondering exactly what kind of music this amazing record would play.

Collingbourne Kingston, Wiltshire, England. August 2005. Borage crop, approximately 200 feet

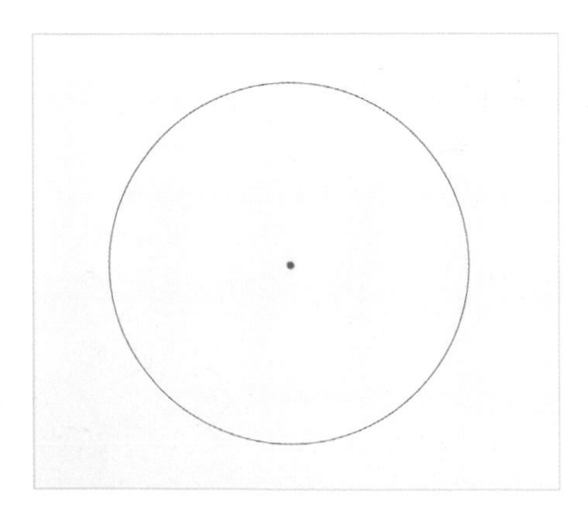

THE CIRCLE AND THE POINT

Before a circle can be drawn, a point has to be established around which the circle can be constructed. Although for our own purposes we may mark that point with a pencil, in reality, the point has no dimension and is known only by inference. The point is the timeless, still centre around which all of creation is formed. The compass should be swung around in one continuous movement, to symbolize the fact that the circle represents unity and one-ness. Ideally, the beginning and end of the circle should not be visible, as a circle has neither beginning nor end, it is eternal. The construction of the circle is the beginnning point of the sacred geometry journey.

The Ridgeway, Wiltshire, England. July 2005. Wheat crop, approximately 200 feet

BECKHAMPTON, 2003

Another variation on the theme of nested rings appeared at Beckhampton in 2003. Notice the incredibly narrow line that marks the perimeter of this circle; it was barely a foot's width. A fine line of flattened crop stems was found inside and most people simply could not walk within the line for fear of damaging this incredibly delicate feature. A similarly fine line is to be found close to the centre of the circle. Another feature of this beautiful formation is the tiny circle just outside the perimeter of the outer ring; it was barely two feet across, and beautifully swirled. The only way to access the individual rings of the formation was via the tractor lines in the field, without which it would have been impossible to walk around inside this formation without damaging the design.

Beckhampton, Wiltshire, England. July 2003. Wheat crop, approximately 200 feet

TWO: THE DIVISION OF UNITY

DYAD – THE *VESICA PISCIS*

Like the splitting of the atom or the Big Bang, the second act of sacred geometry splits apart that which was whole and perfect, in order to bring creation into being. For if there is only unity and wholeness, there can never be diversity and variety. Amidst this primordial schism, the 'one' begins to divide; like the first division of the human egg, a self-similar circle is brought into being and the 'one' becomes 'two'.

On the geometer's drawing board, the point of the compass is placed on the perimeter of the original circle. Keeping the compass open at the same dimension, a second circle of equal size is transcribed, the perimeter of which runs directly through the centre (or crosses the heart) of the first circle. The operation complete, it can now be seen that an almond shape has been created by the two interlocking circles. This almond shape is traditionally known as the *vesica piscis* meaning 'fish bladder' and it is this opening from whence all the rest of creation will be birthed. However, as a consequence of this archetypal rupture, all oppositions now come into being: Light and Dark, Order and Chaos, and of course, in conjunction with the dawn of the concept of Good, its twin Evil is born.

Ashbury, Oxford, England. July 1996. Wheat crop, approximately 200 feet

The interior of Ashbury

ASHBURY, 1996

The *vesica* was first overtly depicted by the crop circle phenomenon in 1996. The wonderful formation at Ashbury allowed one to stand inside the almond-shaped space, from which geometers believe all of creation is birthed. A lovely circle existed at the formation's centre, created only by the lay of the crop, subtly indicating the centre of the design.

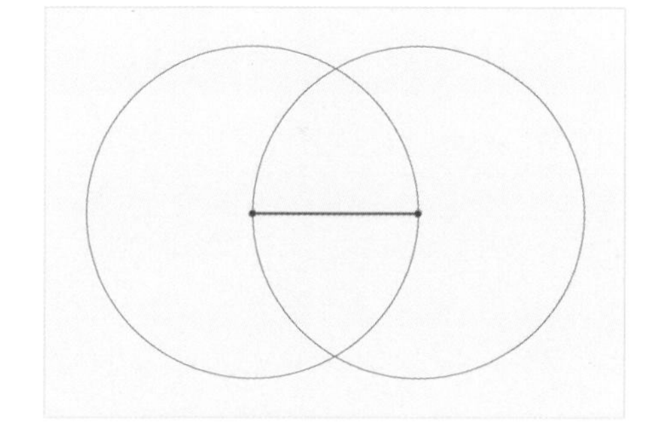

EXPRESSIONS OF TWO-NESS

The *vesica piscis* (left) is the archetypal expression of two-ness, as this is how geometers depict the splitting of one into two. However, two-ness can be expressed in many other ways.

A line is drawn between the two sides of the *vesica* (left). The line is also a product of two-ness as it signifies two points and joins them together.

HOBSON, 2000

This double formation at Hobson is yet another way of expressing two-ness – two formations which appear in the same field on the same night. There have been several instances of this over the years – some larger and more complex than this pair.

(BELOW) Hobson, Wiltshire, England. July 2000. Wheat crop approximately 200 feet

(ABOVE) Marden, Wiltshire, England. August 2005. Wheat crop, approximately 200 feet

MARDEN, 2005

The stunning formation at Marden was another variation on the *vesica* theme. This time, only the central almond-shape is portrayed; the two circles which created it are invisible. Inside, a wonderful eighteen-point lotus-like flower appear four rows of eighteen petals (ever decreasing in size), giving an overall count of seventy-two petals.

Furze Hill, Wiltshire, England. June 1998. Wheat crop, approximately 150 feet

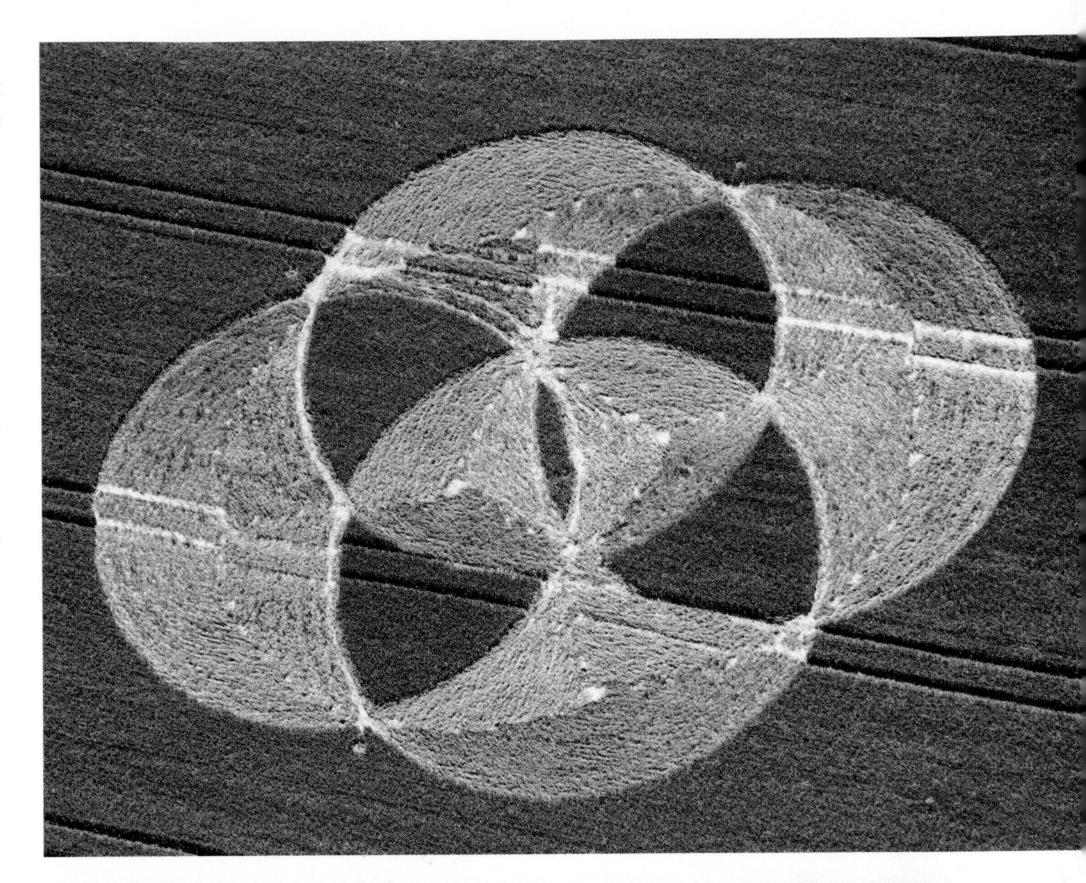

FURZE HILL AND FYFIELD DOWN, 1998

Another important expression of two-ness is that of the twin, or 'twinning'. During 1998, two formations appeared that were clearly related to one another: they were essentially the same size, and each was an inversion of the other. These 'cats-eye' formations appeared in two different crops (wheat and barley), giving a further difference of texture to each formation. Twinning can take two forms, identical and non-identical twins. This pair were clearly non-identical, whereas the pair of dolphins (page 118) are of the identical variety.

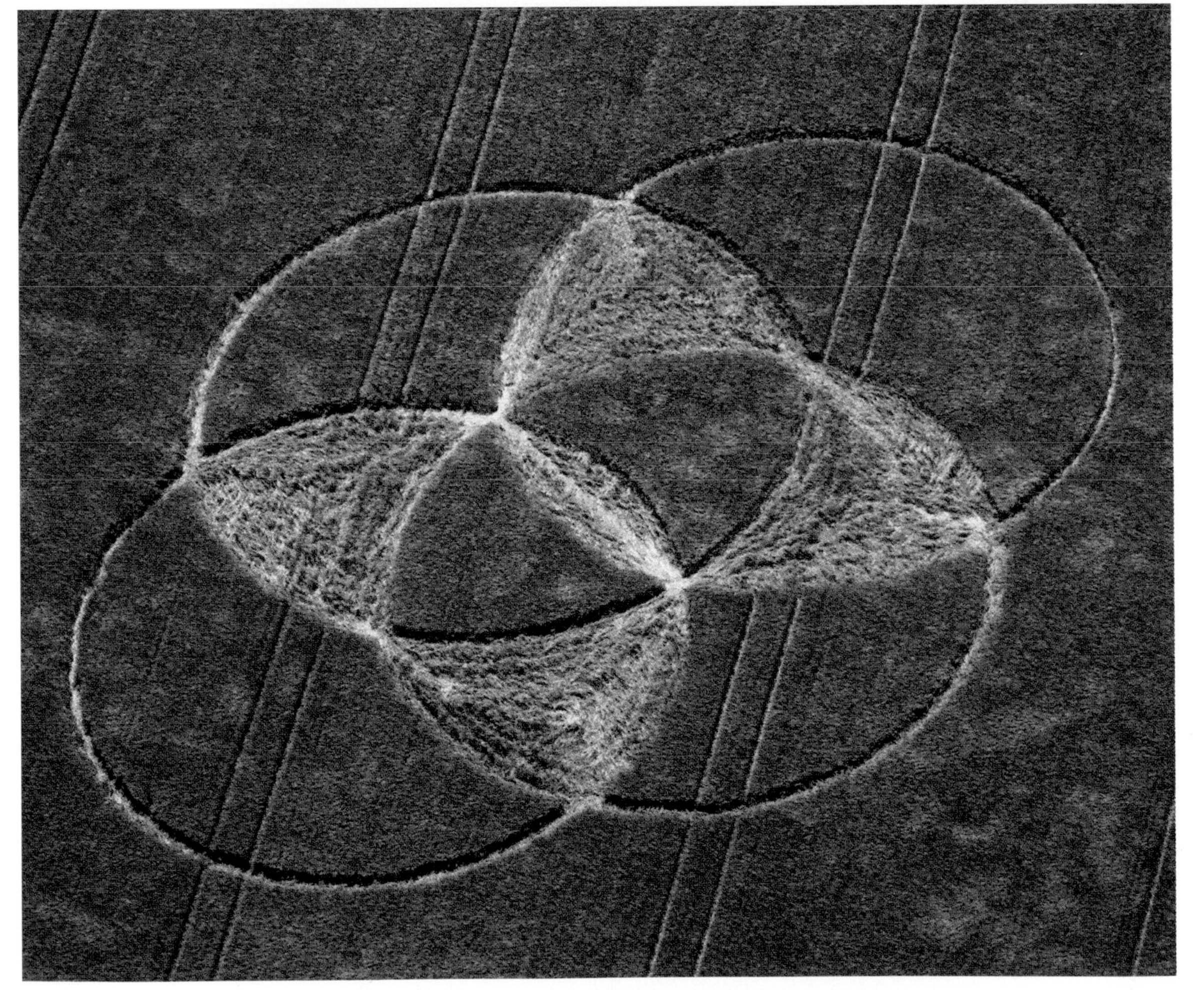

Fyfield Down, Wiltshire, England. June 1998. Barley crop, approximately 150 feet

THREE: TRINITY

TRIAD – THE TRIANGLE

Three is the product of one and two (1 + 2 = 3). The role of three is, unsurprisingly, three-fold. Three simultaneously pierces, balances and then transcends polarity.

The numbers one, two and three are themselves seen as a group, with three signifying the completion of this first phase of creation. The equilateral triangle is the form that breaks through the *vesica* created by its archetypal parents and opens up the birth channel for other numbers to follow.

'I am the One that is Two, that is Three'; this lovely phrase describes how the first three numbers are considered to be a unity themselves. The Christian Trinity – God the Father, God the Son and God the Holy Spirit – is an expression of the tri-fold nature of God and another example of the inherent trinity in unity.

Three restores a sense of balance to our sacred numbers. Three resolves the tension of the dyad (opposites), by creating a pattern of 'beginning, middle and end'. The appearance of unity is restored, but of course it is now three-fold rather than a single unity.

The process of transition from two to three is very important to us as human beings. Often we seek to resolve tension and conflict within ourselves and, if we are successful, we say we have been able to change ourselves. What is crucial for a change of this nature to occur is an ability to see things from a different perspective, or in balanced proportion; this ultimately is what breaks the endless dyad of conflict. However, we don't suddenly become a totally different person – we are essentially the same, but simultaneously also a little different.

We could say that we have been able to restore our inner unity and resolve our conflict, by finding a different (third) perspective on things.

Another example of the principle of three-ness is found in the court room, where we have the opposing councils of prosecutor and defence, and the judge who sits between them (often in a triangular arrangement).

This example also illustrates how the introduction of a third element naturally provides a place for perspective. The triangle provides a third point from which both sides of the dyad can be seen in perfect proportion.

Finally, the arrival of three is also the first act of evolution. Evolution transcends what has come before to manifest something that is at root the same but also simultaneously different and new. Often when we have resolved a part of our inner conflict we feel renewed, and might feel we are a better person for it – this is personal evolution.

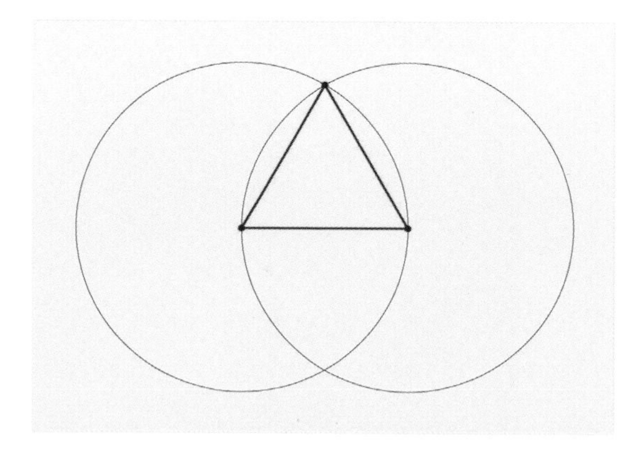

The triangle is born from within the vesica. *Using the line that connects the two sides of the* vesica *together, connect each end of that line to the apex of the* vesica. *This creates an equilateral triangle.*

Liddington Castle, Wiltshire, England. June 2001. Wheat crop, approximately 200 feet

Liddington Castle, 2001

This formation uses three interlocking circles (or crescents) enclosed within a circle, to create a tri-fold unity. At the centre of the formation, a triangle is created with convex sides. Patterns akin to this have been used in the 'trefoil' design of church windows for centuries, representing the trinity, or tri-fold nature of God.

Expressions of Three-ness

Three-ness can be expressed either as a three-fold unity – as three interconnecting rings, or perhaps as three circles contained by an outer ring – or as an entirely new shape, the equilateral triangle, whose three sides and three angles are all in perfect proportion.

BERWICK BASSETT, 2001

This magnificent formation in a field of young, emerald-coloured barley was a play on something called 'curves of pursuit'. Each successive convex triangle, whilst receding in size, simutaneously rotates several degrees, creating curves which seem eternally to pursue each other.

Berwick Bassett, Wiltshire, England. June 2001. Barley crop, approximately 200 feet

Avebury Trusloe, Wiltshire, England. August 1998. Wheat crop, approximately 150 feet

AVEBURY TRUSLOE, 1998

This stunning formation is one of only two to have appeared solely as a true triangle shape. The design is nicely finished off with three tiny circles at the apex of each point. Interestingly, the crop is all laid in one direction, rather than swirled in the more familiar circular pattern.

BLACKLANDS, 2004

This simple but elegant three-fold formation (below) also uses the repetition of a single shape at different scales.

Blacklands, Wiltshire, England. August 2004. Wheat crop, approximately 100 feet

Picked Hill, Wiltshire, England. July 2000.
Barley crop, approximately 180 feet

PICKED HILL, 2000

The formation at Picked Hill was a more traditional three-fold design. It contained three groups of three different-shaped petals – as if reinforcing its very three-ness.

BROAD HINTON, 2003

This crop formation (below) was based on the famous 'Flower of Life' design, venerated for many years. Essentially, the Flower of Life is a set of interlocking circles, which are said to contain all the geometrical designs used in creation. Here, the interlocking pattern has been selectively used to fill in the central space of this triangular formation.

Broad Hinton, Wiltshire, England. July 2003. Wheat crop, approximately 150 feet

Lockeridge, Wiltshire, England. July 2000. Wheat crop, approximately 200 feet

LOCKERIDGE, 2000

A three-armed propeller-type design, this crop circle combines the circle, the triangle and three narrow almond-shaped arms. This formation appeared on a naturally sloping field and was visible to anyone and everyone driving by.

Winterbourne Bassett, Wiltshire, England. June 1997. Barley crop, approximately 200 feet

Winterbourne Bassett, 1997

This is an all-time classic crop formation. The striking harlequin-like design is highlighted by the fantastic green of the young barley in which it appeared. Taken the morning on which this formation first appeared, the photograph captures the way the early morning sun reflects like quicksilver on the freshly laid crop.

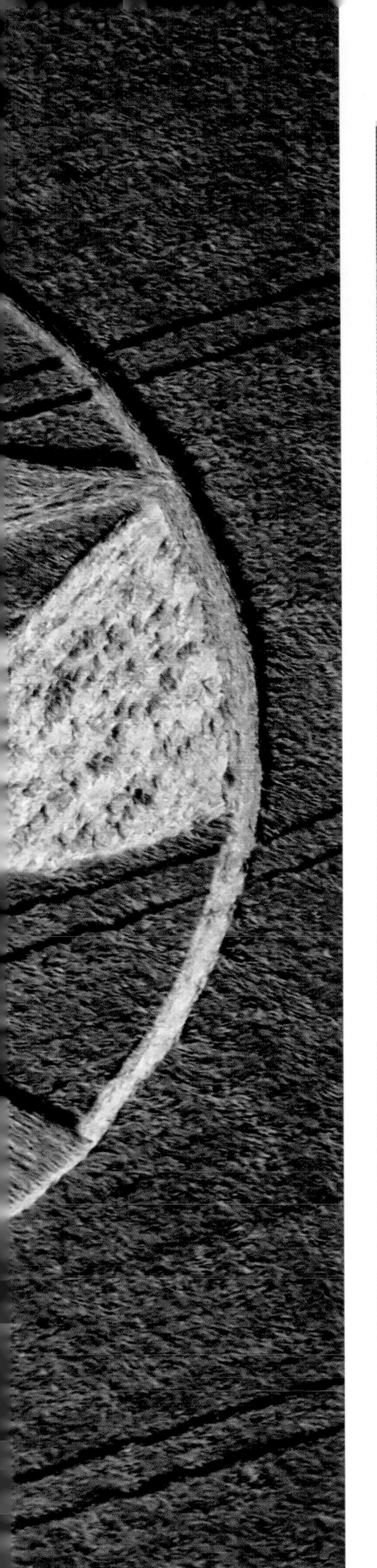

Giant's Grave, Oare, Wiltshire, England. August 2000. Wheat crop, approximately 200 feet

GIANT'S GRAVE, 2000

Another arrangement of three circles, bound together by a fourth – this formation was interesting because two of the arms are identical but the third is slightly different – yet another expression of three-ness.

WEST TISTED, 2000

West Tisted is, without doubt, one of the most beautiful three-fold formations to date. An undulating necklace of small, round wheat pearls, locked in place by a narrow ring.

West Tisted, Hampshire, England. July 2000. Wheat crop, approximately 200 feet

FOUR: THE FOUR PILLARS OF MATERIAL REALITY

TETRAD – THE SQUARE AND CUBE

With four we move away from the archetypal and perfected realm, to begin the creation of material reality as we know it. With the arrival of four, depth and volume are brought into being; in other words, our three-dimensional reality becomes possible.

The shape of four is the square (or the cube). Both the square and the cube exhibit stability, equality and strength, all attributes of four-ness. Four is also the number that will give physical form to everything that now comes into being; physical matter is the necessary protective clothing for everything that will exist in the new material realm. Four represents matter, substance and mass, the primary building blocks of the universe, and also the four classical elements, Earth, Air, Fire and Water.

Carl Jung, the renowned psychoanalyst, postulated that our inner self was quadratic in form: he called it the 'quaternity of the self'– thinking, feeling, sensing and intuition. The act of dividing the square into four quarters is almost instinctual. Mandalas (often considered visual representations of the inner self) are also often quadratic in form.

With the birth of four, we also find ourselves back at square one. To the Ancient Greeks, four was the first true number; with four we are beginning a new phase, hence the relationship between one and four.

However, there is also another more mystical connection between one and four, which has been used by temple and church builders for thousands of years, and it is known as the 'Squaring of the Circle'.

The crop circles have used squares, cubes and creations of four-ness to produce some beautiful formations.

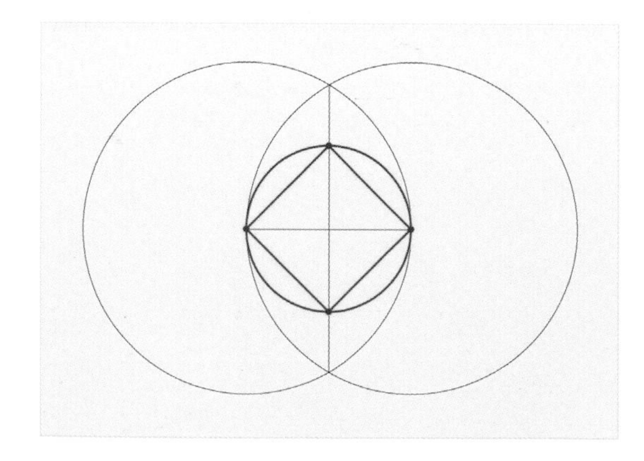

A circle is drawn which fits exactly the dimension of the centre of the vesica. *Using both the original line across the width of the* vesica *and a further line joining the two apexes of the* vesica *as a guide, a square can be drawn inside the circle. The birth of the square also ushers in the third dimension, the point, width, height and breadth.*

Lurkeley Hill, Wiltshire, England. June 2005. Wheat crop, approximately 200 feet

LURKELEY HILL, 2005

A personal favourite, this lovely formation combines classical four-fold geometry – the division of the circle by the four cardinal points – with that of the *vesica*. Eight vesica shapes (two groups of four) guide the positioning of the smaller circles that are not involved in marking the quadrants of the design. This formation combines the numbers, two, four, eight and twelve.

Monkton Down, Wiltshire, England. June 2005. Wheat crop, approximately 200 feet

MONKTON DOWN, 2005

Circles also play a central role in this design to form a square shape. Twenty-five circles of equal diameter are nestled together like a group of pool or snooker balls. Four of the balls seem to be missing, or are of a different colour or texture, creating yet another cross-shape.

Honey Street, Wiltshire, England. July 1999. Wheat crop, approximately 200 feet

HONEY STREET, 1999

Another cube-shaped formation at Honey Street appeared during the summer of 1999. On this occasion the cube also had a sphere suspended within it.

Allington Down, 1999

The birth of four-ness ushers in the third dimension and the cube, and there have been several cuboid patterns to appear as crop circles. This stunning example at Allington Down recalled the work of the artist M. C. Esher, famous for his use of shapes to create optical illusions, and the ingenious repeated tiling of patterns and shapes in the creation of larger unrelated designs.

(LEFT AND BELOW) *Allington Down, Wiltshire, England. June 1999. Wheat crop, approximately 200 feet*

Inside Allington Down

(RIGHT AND BELOW) *Marden, Wiltshire, England. August 2005. Wheat crop, approximately 200 feet*

MARDEN, 2005 AND EVERLEIGH ASHES, 2000

Although the Celtic cross (or quintuplet) has five dots, it is in fact an archetypal expression of four-ness, as its geometry is four-fold. Many designs of this type have appeared throughout the years, but these two examples are of particular note. At Everleigh Ashes, the central circle was replaced by a tumulus (an ancient burial mound), whilst at Marden the centre circle was filled with exquisite knots and leaves.

(FAR RIGHT) *Everleigh Ashes, Wiltshire, England. July 2000. Wheat crop, approximately 200 feet*

(BELOW) *The interior of Marden's middle ring*

(ABOVE AND BELOW) *Etchilhampton, Wiltshire, England. August 1997. Wheat crop, approximately 175 feet*

Etchilhampton, 1997

The 'grid' formations were yet another expression of four-ness. The grid at Etchilhampton was in fact one of two formations to appear in that field on the same night. Another six-armed spinner design had appeared close by, and the two were undoubtedly a pair. This formation was found to be 26 squares one side by 30 squares on the other. It was speculated that if the 26 squares represented weeks, they would represent a half year period. If we multiply the 30 squares by 0.5 years, we get 15 years. The formation appeared in 1997, adding our 15 years takes us to 2012 – the end of the Ancient Mayan calendar! So this formation could be a calendrical grid.

EAST KENNETT, 2000

Another stunning grid–type formation appeared close to the chambered long barrow at West Kennett. This time the square grid was also further split into four sections, by alternating the sizes of the small squares and oblongs which comprised the grid area. This formation, like its Etchilhampton counterpart, was utterly incomprehensible from the ground. Whilst crop circles are often labyrinthine and temple-like on the ground, they are undoubtedly meant to be viewed from the air. Interestingly, in both these formations the interior grid-workings were unconsciously forbidding to the visitor; almost all walked around the giant squares, unwilling to penetrate the intricate inner design.

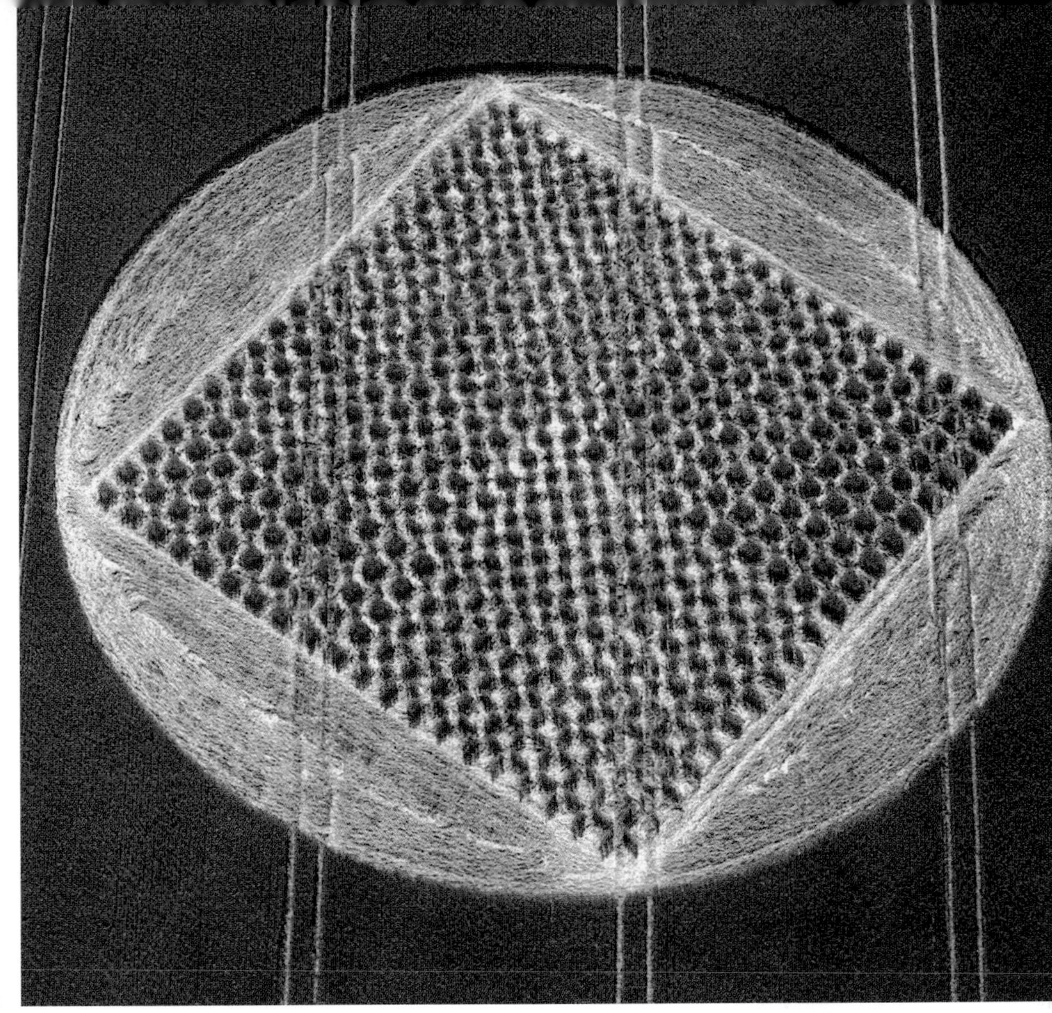

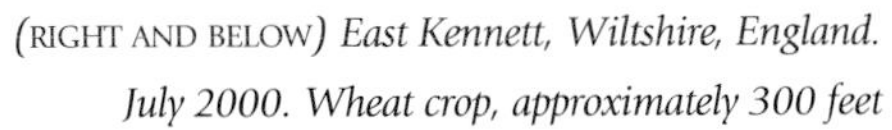

(RIGHT AND BELOW) *East Kennett, Wiltshire, England. July 2000. Wheat crop, approximately 300 feet*

FIVE: THE MYSTERY OF LIFE

PENTAD – THE PENTAGON AND PENTAGRAM

Five is perhaps one of the most mysterious and misunderstood of numbers and it has a myriad of properties. Four has created material reality and the world, matter, substance and mass. With the birth of five, the mysterious gift of life is breathed into that world.

It has often been called the Quintessence, meaning 'fifth-being'. It is that mysterious something that animates matter to life, without which creation would be barren – five brings meaning into the world, through life. Five is a number that resonates powerfully with us. Five-fold geometry governs the human form – a head, two arms and two legs. We also have five fingers on each hand and five toes on each foot. However, five is not just found throughout the human body, it is found throughout the natural world, most prevalently in living forms.

The shapes of five-ness are the pentagon and the pentagram. The pentagon has five equal sides and angles, whilst the pentagram is a five-pointed star. The pentagram has a somewhat chequered history, and is often associated with witchcraft and the dark arts. Reverse a pentagram and many see a symbol resembling a two-horned devil – this is unfortunate, and makes the pentagram a most misunderstood and sometimes taboo shape.

The true nature of the pentagram is to do with the mystery of the greatest of all gifts – life. It is also about the propagation of life. The pentagram has some extraordinary regenerative properties. Many progressively smaller pentagram stars can be fitted inside a larger one – regeneration through self-symmetry or self-similarity is an important property of all life on the planet. It gives the pentagram star almost fractal-like abilities; fractals are shapes that mimic natural systems and are generated through self-similarity (see page 144).

The pentagram star also generates one of the most mysterious and important geometrical proportions, the Golden Section, also known as the Divine Proportion (see page 84). It is also the generator of the famous Fibonacci Sequence, a series of numbers that is found in living systems throughout nature, in which each successive number is the sum of the preceding two. Using this sequence, Fibonacci showed that nature used a principle of generation-from-within in order to propagate living forms.

The Golden Section/Fibonacci Sequence can also be found in the form of the Golden Spiral. The crop circles have used the pentagram star, the Golden Section and the Golden Spiral in their designs, making manifest in the crop fields the very secrets of life.

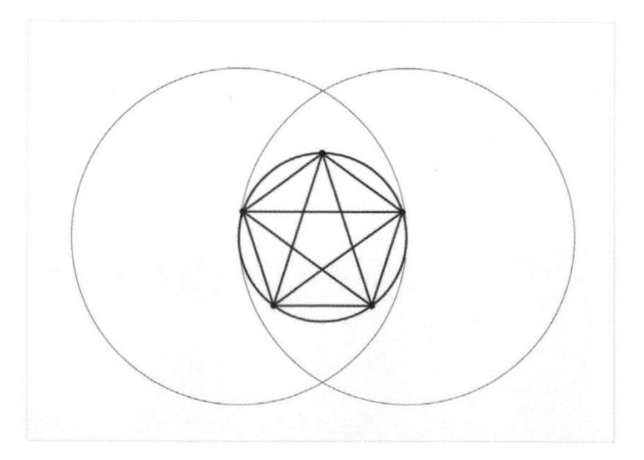

The birth of the pentagram from within the vesica *is a slightly more complicated proposition than the triangle or the square. It uses both the line that connects the two sides of the* vesica *and the circle which fits exactly inside. It then takes a further nine steps to create the pentagram within the circle using a compass.*

Bishops Cannings, Wiltshire, England. July 1997. Wheat crop, approximately 200 feet

BISHOPS CANNINGS, 1997

The arrival of this magical star heralded the beginning of a series of five-pointed stars (pentagrams) over the next season or so. The first pentagram had been at Bythorn in Cambridgeshire in 1993, but it had not appeared again until this formation in 1997. This crop circle was beautifully constructed with cookie-cutter precision and was striking when viewed from the air. Its simple, clean lines left no room for doubt that exploration of five-ness had begun in earnest.

(ABOVE AND BELOW) *Avebury Trusloe, Wiltshire, England. June 1998. Wheat crop, approximately 200 feet*

AVEBURY TRUSLOE, 1998

1998 saw a whole series of pentagram star crop circles. The first of the year was this lovely pentagram enclosed within a ten-petalled flower. Note the way the crop is flattened between each arm of the star, creating a wonderful effect from the air of shade and light. There is something mirror-like about the way the sunlight reflects from the interior of some of these formations – as though they are suspended on a pool of quicksilver or gold.

DADFORD, 1998

As the summer of 1998 unfolded, the pentagram formations began to evolve. This formation occurred close to the famous F1 motor racing track at Silverstone – home of the British Grand Prix. This time we were given two interlocking pentagram stars instead of the familiar single star. Accompanying them were three tiny and curious glyphs. One is clearly an Egyptian ankh; the other two are less distinct, although there was much speculation about the centre glyph being reminiscent of Ganesha the Hindu elephant deity.

Dadford, Buckinghamshire, England. July 1998. Wheat crop, approximately 200 feet

BECKHAMPTON, 1998

Yet another pentagram formation appeared towards the end of the 1998 season. Once again two interlocking pentagram stars feature. However, this time the top star is smaller than the lower one. Both are locked together by a pentagon shape and enclosed within a containing circle – a beautiful expression of five-ness.

(ABOVE AND RIGHT) *Beckhampton, Wiltshire, England. August 1998. Wheat crop, approximately 200 feet*

GREEN STREET, AVEBURY, 2003

As an expression of five-ness there can be no bettering the formation at Green Street: an outer pentagon, with interior pentagrams, the iteration of five-ness is all-pervading. There are some other lovely numbers at play in this formation – seven pentagram stars in total, giving this formation an ineffable quality, and in addition to the two pentagons (one containing the stars, the other enclosing the whole design) an overall number of nine is achieved, which is a number of completion and conclusion. Through the geometry and numbers encoded in the crop circles we can discern the nuances and subtleties in the design, and glimpse their inner meanings. Numbers have qualities as well as quantities.

Green Street, Avebury, Wiltshire, England. July 2003. Wheat crop, approximately 350 feet

(RIGHT AND BELOW)
Barbury Castle, Wiltshire, England. April 1997. Oilseed rape (canola) crop, approximately 200 feet

BARBURY CASTLE, 1997

Although often obvious, crop circle geometry also has a hidden side. This beautiful collection of six moons around a central circle and ring might quite legitimately be interpreted as having the properties of six-ness. However, whilst this is quite true, it also has a hidden (or esoteric) five-fold geometry as shown in the diagram below, drawn by crop circle researcher and geometer Michael Glickman.

SIX: ECONOMY AND EFFICIENCY

HEXAD – THE HEXAGON AND HEXAGRAM

With four having created the elemental world, and five animating those elements, six is about the organization and utilization of those elements and living forms. With the introduction of six come the important tenets of economy and efficiency. The shapes of six-ness are the hexagon and the hexagram.

In modern society, economy and efficiency can be bywords for meanness and cost-, corner-, or job- cutting, but in the natural world, getting the most from precious natural resources is essential and therefore underpins the design and structure of many of nature's forms.

In a world where resources are finite, ensuring optimal yield (efficiency) from all materials also ensures the greatest longevity of those resources and ultimately of the living systems they support. Economy and efficiency of this kind are about more, rather than less – they are about the continuing long-term survival of life and the environment that supports it. We could learn much from observing and learning from the economy and efficiency of form in nature.

The structure of the honeycomb nicely illustrates this philosophy at work. Hexagons lock together perfectly so that there is no space between them; this means that as a group of storage compartments, the hexagons provide the largest possible capacity, whilst using the least amount of materials and labour. When hexagon shapes are built into a structure they share external faces, making the building process extremely efficient. The hexagon shape brings a further property to the structure, and that is strength: the regularity of the shape brings stability and strength to structures which contain it.

The strength of six-ness is perhaps best demonstrated by the changing of water into ice. As water molecules cool, they tighten into hexagonal patterns where they form the basis for six-sided snowflakes. The colder the molecules become the more they bond together. The six-fold symmetry of the molecular bonds helps to make ice an extremely strong and hard substance.

Crop circles have explored six-ness in many different ways, but it is interesting to note that whilst there have been many six-fold formations, and many hexagon shapes, for some reason hexagrams have seldom been seen.

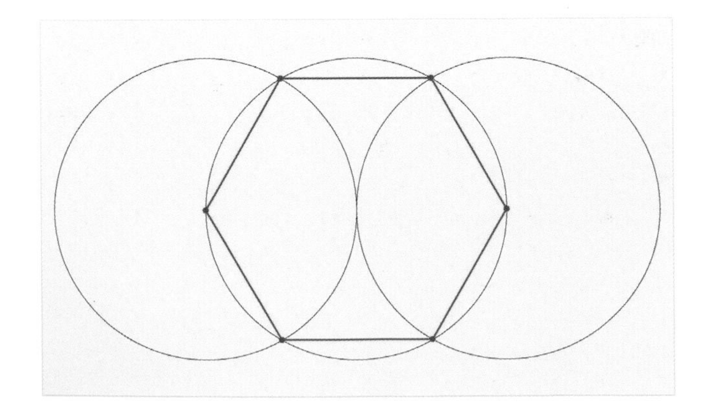

In contrast to the pentagram, the creation of a hexagon is much simpler. Three circles of equal size are drawn together (as shown) and the connections between the three define the points needed to create a perfect hexagram shape.

Warminster, Wiltshire, England. July 1997. Wheat crop, approximately 300 feet

Warminster, 1997

This massive hexagonal formation appeared below Clay Hill, a location synonymous with UFO sightings in the 1970s. A wonderful view could be had of this formation by climbing up the hill and looking down into the field below. A standing hexagon shape is enclosed within a containing circle. The central star-like shape has twelve points, each with three lines emanating towards the perimeter of the designcircle. Many likened this design to the spokes of a bicycle wheel.

WINDMILL HILL, 2005

The marvellous hexagon at Windmill Hill explored the relationship between the triangle and the hexagon. Interestingly, the design contains thirty-six equilateral triangles (twenty-four outlined triangles and twelve smaller standing triangles: 24 + 12 = 36). Six is the square root of thirty six, which is the number of sides in a hexagon.

Windmill Hill, Wiltshire, England. June 2005. Wheat crop, approximately 180 feet

Littlebury Green, Essex, England. July 1996. Barley crop, approximately 200 feet

LITTLEBURY GREEN, 1996

The meticulous precision of this formation was sublime and makes it one of the most beautiful crop circles of all time. The simple economy and regularity of design expresses six-ness exquisitely.

ALL CANNINGS, 2000

The All Cannings flower is another inventive expression of six-ness and, as we progress through the numbers, it becomes possible to see how much interplay between shapes and numbers can be at work within a single formation. It also explains why the pursuit of the crop circles can be so thoroughly absorbing and exciting – watching and waiting to see how the shapes will unfold and develop each year.

All Cannings, Wiltshire, England. August 2000. Wheat crop, approximately 100 feet

AVEBURY HENGE, 2005

You might say that this gigantic cereological necklace is strung with hexagonal pearls of wisdom. One of the most ambitious and accomplished designs based around six-ness, this wonderful crop circle attracted thousands of curious visitors the summer it appeared. A magical exploration of the relationship between the triangle and the hexagon – notice the six-pointed hexagram at the centre of the formation, made entirely from equilateral triangles.

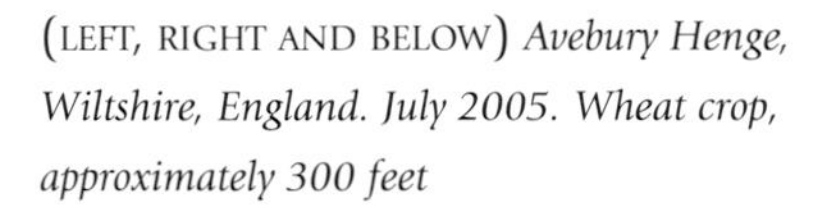

(LEFT, RIGHT AND BELOW) *Avebury Henge, Wiltshire, England. July 2005. Wheat crop, approximately 300 feet*

Cherhill, Wiltshire, England. August 2005. Wheat crop, approximately 200 feet

CHERHILL, 2005

The hexagon of all hexagons appeared below Oldbury Castle, at Cherhill. Thirty-one individual hexagons comprised this amazing formation. 2005 turned out to be a year of hexagons, with many appearing in formations that summer.

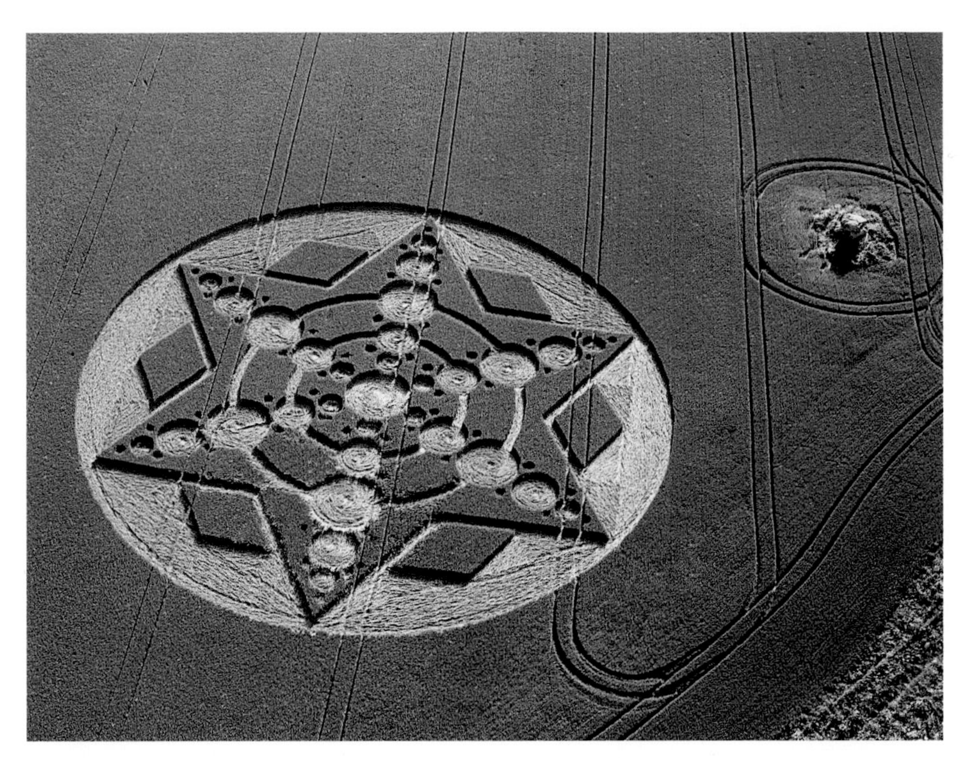

DEVIL'S DEN, 1999

Devil's Den is thought to be the stone remnants of a long barrow (ancient burial mound). However, stones of this type are more commonly referred to as 'dolmens'. The formation that appeared alongside the stones was a rare six-pointed star. The night it appeared, there was a power failure in the nearby village; this formation also had strange electrical and magnetic properties that affected mobile phones and cameras – but only whilst inside the circle.

(LEFT AND BELOW) *Devil's Den, Wiltshire, England. July 1999. Wheat crop, approximately 250 feet*

SEVEN: THE MYSTERIOUS FEMININE

HEPTAD – THE HEPTAGON AND HEPTAGRAMS

Just when we think all is structured according to best economy, efficiency and order, we come face to face with the mysterious and beautiful number seven – the number of the colours in the rainbow, the notes of the musical scale and, of course, the seven deadly sins. However, seven is often considered a lucky number.

Of all the numbers from one to ten, seven is the only number that will not divide equally into the 360° of the circle (the monad) and the only number that cannot be born from the *vesica*. The division of a circle into seven parts produces an 'irrational number' (a number whose decimal places would stretch into infinity without ever finding a whole number resolution), and it is these particular properties that give seven its association with the feminine and, more specifically, the mysterious virginal feminine.

Perhaps in an unintentional play on words, the 'irrational' of 'irrational number' links us with this ancient view of the feminine principle. The feminine was synonymous with the irrational, the unconscious, with dreams, intuitions and the deep waters of the emotional self.

The unconscious is the root of that archetypal chaotic and unpredictable element, without which diversity, variety and evolution could not exist. Too much order leads to sterility and stagnation; a little chaos is absolutely necessary in order to precipitate change. Just as man needs woman in order to propagate the human race, order needs a little chaos to generate a continuing unfolding creation. Order is needed to balance and harmonize, chaos is needed to unbalance and de-harmonize – without it the world would be sterile and lifeless.

However, seven is a 'whole' of sorts: as already noted, it governs the notes of the musical scale, the colours of the rainbow (or colours of refracted light), and the number of major chakras (subtle energy centres in the body). Because of its connection with such numinous phenomena (music, light and subtle energy) seven is the number of spirit.

There have been a series of seven-fold (or seven-element) formations over the years. They occupy a special place in crop circle history, often as mysterious as the number which governs their form.

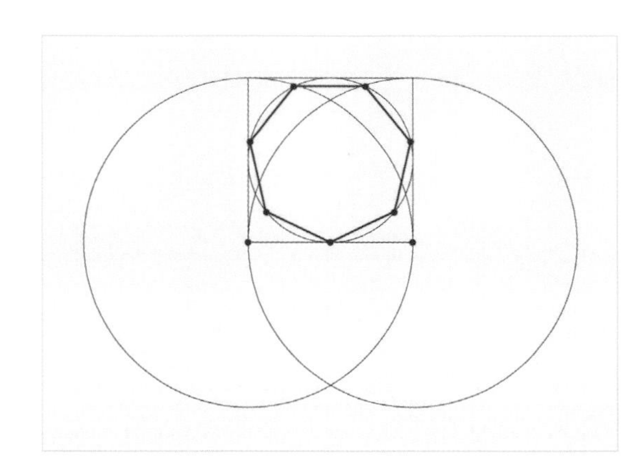

THE BIRTH OF SEVEN

Seven is the only number (from one to ten) that cannot be divided equally into the 360° of the circle. The Heptagon is born from outside the *vesica*, above the apex of the almond shape (see above).

Greek mythology tells us that Athene (Goddess of seven-ness) was born from the forehead of Zeus, who had swallowed his lover Metis whole. Zeus subsequently developed a terrible headache, his head was split open and Athene emerged, fully grown.

Danebury Ring, Hampshire, England. July 1998. Wheat crop, approximately 150 feet

DANEBURY RING, 1998

This lovely formation was the first true seven-fold formation to appear. There is something about the design which suggests an anti-clockwise spin and gives a slightly disharmonious edge to the image. This could be taken as a visual clue as to its unusual seven-fold geometry.

Unlike the pentagram (five) or the hexagram (six), once we reach seven, two star patterns become possible. The stars are created by connecting every two corners and every three corners of the heptagon respectively.

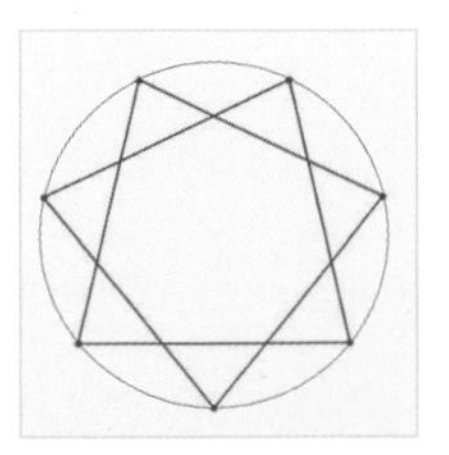

EAST FIELD, 1998

1998 was also the year of seven, with three seven-fold formations appearing. The beautiful green of the young barley crop and the shadows and highlights created by the lay of the crop gave this shape an almost organic feel.

On the morning of its appearance, the lines and tiny outer circles were perfect, but over the course of the day and overnight a wind and rain storm damaged the delicate perimeter design (as seen in the picture below). The centre was a beautifully woven knot of crop. This formation holds the record for the largest expanse of flattened crop – 1.6 acres.

(LEFT, BELOW LEFT AND BELOW)
East Field, Alton Barnes, Wiltshire, England. July 1998. Barley crop, approximately 300 feet

At the centre of East Field was a carefully woven knot of crop

(ABOVE AND BELOW) *Tawsmead Copse, Wiltshire, England. August 1998. Wheat crop, approximately 350 feet*

TAWSMEAD COPSE, 1998

One of the final circles of 1998 was the wonderful seven-fold design at Tawsmead Copse. Upon entering this formation we noticed, just within its perimeter, a neat row of walking shoes and trainers: people had felt the need to remove their shoes before walking around any further. This was a fascinating automatic response to this crop circle and expresses succinctly the unique atmosphere these spaces can unconsciously provoke within the individual. The floor lay of this circle was exquisite, truly like flowing water; one almost had the sense of movement sitting amongst the fallen wheat. This formation was undeniably temple-like in its effect upon the psyche and many sat with us in a quiet kind of reverence to watch the sunset.

ROUNDWAY, 1999

The most fantastic seven-fold design to date has to be the 'Roundway Splash'. This incredible double seven-pointed star, with circles upon each point, was an extraordinary space to experience. The formation measured approximately 300-350 feet in diameter and once again, contained an incredible volume of flattened crop. It certainly supports the thought that 'big circles = big power' – the largest formations certainly convey a sense of magnificence and sheer power.

Roundway, Wiltshire, England. July 1999. Wheat crop, approximately 350 feet

HERN AIRPORT, 2001

Never was there a better photo opportunity for a crop circle. Located at the end of the runway at Hern Airport was this strange little seven-fold pattern, formed in the ripening yellow of an oilseed rape (canola) field.

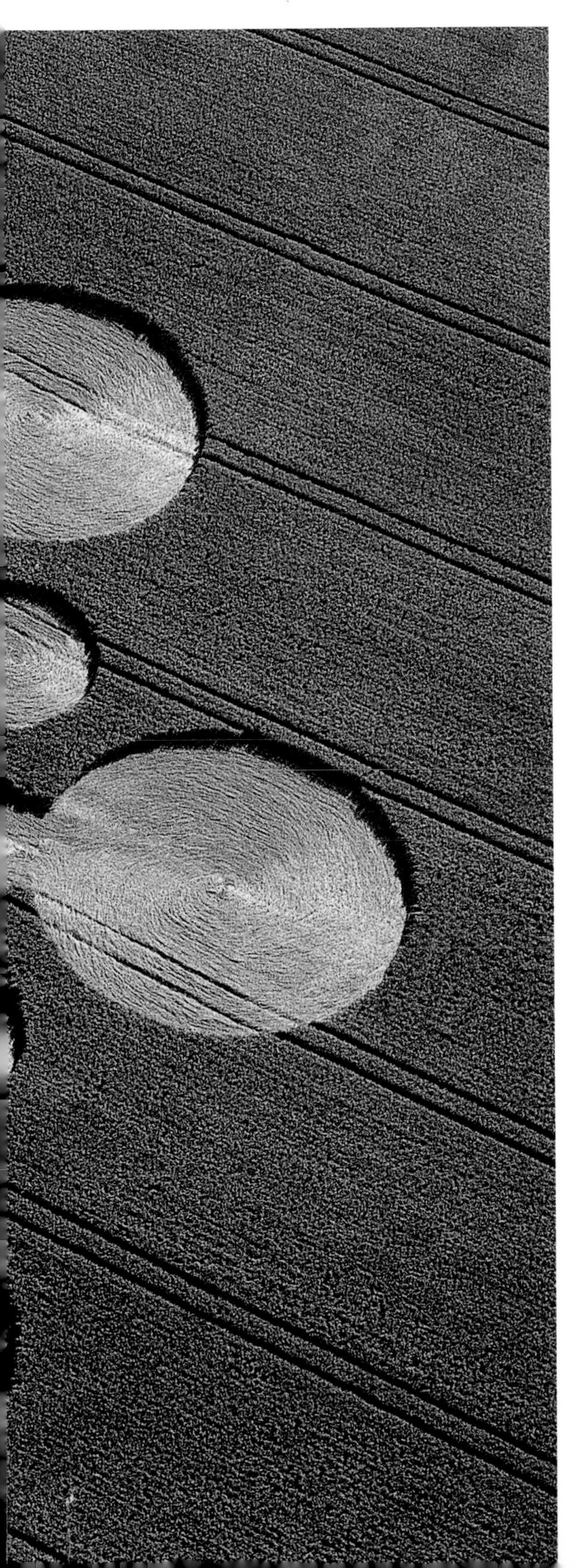

Hern Airport, Dorset, England. May 2001. Oilseed rape (canola) crop, approximately 150 feet

EIGHT: RESONANCE AND HARMONICS

OCTAD – THE OCTAGON AND OCTOGRAM

Having established the seven notes of the musical scale, the introduction of eight would signify the sounding of the octave. With the octave (*oct*-ave), we have the birth of resonance and harmonics.

It would be useful to think of crop circle designs as harmonic and resonant in the musical sense. Often they combine the geometry of different numbers to create beautiful synergies; frozen symphonies of shape and number.

When we play a musical scale on the piano, we play A, B, C, D E, F, G – the seven notes of the musical scale. However, to start the next scale, we find we are playing another A. This A is called the octave. This second A is simultaneously the same as the original A, but it also different - it is separated by pitch.

What makes the octave so important is that it is the end of something, and yet also the beginning of something else. When we play the musical scale, it does not sound complete to only play the seven notes – we have to sound the octave for it to sound complete. But the octave is also the beginning note of a new scale, so the octave is the natural ending of one scale and at the same time the natural beginning of a new one.

This notion of a simultaneous end and beginning is important one in nature and geometry, it is the principle that underlies periodicity in cycles of life and renewal and is the prime principle of eight-ness.

Eight is often seen as a number of renewal or periodicity; the number that signifies the end of one thing and the beginning of another; a change from one state to another. Eight can be interpreted as being resonant of the division of unity: cell mitosis is an eight-stage process, whereby one cell divides and becomes two.

Eight is also seen as a lunar number, with the phases of the moon being traditionally split into eight: Full Moon, Waxing Gibbous, First Quarter, Waxing Crescent, New Moon, Waning Crescent, Last Quarter, Waning Gibbous – and back to Full Moon. This lunar aspect reveals a hidden association between seven and eight: there are approximately seven days between each quarter lunar phase, making the lunar month approximately 28 days.

Resonance also plays a large part in human interaction. We speak of being drawn to friends and colleagues because they share something in common with us; we feel they are on our wavelength. In other words, we find them resonant to ourselves; we are naturally drawn to people who are like us in some way, it makes us feel comfortable and in harmony with others in the human race.

Eight has been explored in crop circle design many times, but most often as an octogram (an eight-pointed star) rather than an octagon.

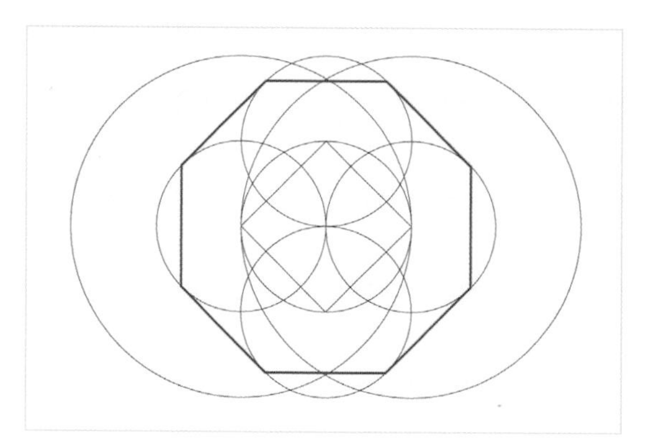

EXPRESSION OF EIGHT-NESS

The octogram can be viewed as an intersection of two squares, and this has been seen in a good few circle designs. However, eight-ness has also been expressed in a number of other ways – as an eight-fold division of the circle, and even as an unfolded octogram. The crop circle at Lane End Down (right) is a lovely example of an eight-fold mandala-like pattern, of which there have been several. The diagram above shows the geometry necessary for the creation of an octagon.

Lane End Down, Hampshire, England. July 2001. Wheat crop, approximately 120 feet

Bishops Cannings, 2000

The eight-fold design at Bishops Cannings is a classic octogram; note the double square shape. This is an interesting photograph because this formation contained a slight imperfection when it first appeared. Most other photographers waited until after the first day to record the formation, at which point the imperfection had disappeared.

Bishops Cannings, Wiltshire, England. June 2000. Wheat crop, approximately 200 feet

The Punchbowl, Cheesefoot Head, Hampshire. July 1995. Oat crop, approximately 300 feet

CHEESEFOOT HEAD, 1995

This magnificent eight-fold design appeared in the famous Punchbowl in Hampshire (a natural amphitheatre). Many early circles occurred in this remarkable location, but the land is no longer farmed and is now used to host an annual music festival. This formation was quickly nicknamed 'The Jellyfish', and is one of a small group of formations to have appeared in an oat crop.

WEST OVERTON, 1999

To some, the formation at West Overton was a Space Station, but to others it was undoubtedly an unfolded octahedron. If you draw up this design and cut it out, you can fold it into the octahedron shape. The octahedron is an object with eight equilateral triangle sides. It is one of the five Platonic Solids – regular solids that have equal sides and identical faces. This is the only time a shape has been depicted in such a way.

West Overton, Wiltshire, England. June 1999. Wheat crop, approximately 250 feet

Huish, Wiltshire, England. August 2001. Wheat crop, approximately 200 feet

HUISH, 2001

This wonderful web-like pattern has circles which are placed at eight equal intervals around its perimeter, but has thirty-three circles all together.

OGBOURNE ST GEORGE, 2003

The magnificent formation at Ogbourne St George was situated in another natural amphitheatre. Whilst this design has only six arms it is unquestionably based on eight-fold geometry – two of the arms seem to have been omitted.

(ABOVE AND BELOW)
Ogbourne St. George, Wiltshire, England. June 2003. Wheat crop, approximately 400 feet

NINE: SUBLIME THRESHOLD

ENNEAD – THE NONAGON AND ENNEAGRAM

If the creation of human life begins with the division of the egg, and after nine months of gestation, the human infant crosses the threshold of the womb and is born into this material world then in many ways, the human life is wonderfully resonant of the geometric principles through which we have now journeyed.

The number nine marks a sublime threshold over which we all cross when we enter this life as a newborn – a brand new potentiality, and simultaneously the highest expression of life on our planet.

Nine is the threshold of numbers and also the culmination of all previous numbers. After nine we travel beyond the decad, onto an entirely new level. Ten is not the last number, rather it the first of a whole new world order.

As with the number seven, it is impossible to draw a perfectly equal nine-sided shape (called a nonagon), or a nine-pointed star (an enneagram), using only the geometer's tools of compass and straight edge, although close approximations are possible. However, unlike seven, nine will divide into the 360° of the circle to give nine divisions of 40°, so with the aid of a protractor to measure angles, the problem does become solvable.

These peculiar properties give nine its dualistic character and are symbolic of its role as a conduit between this material world and other more mysterious states of existence.

In modern times, the enneagram has manifested itself as a psychological tool for the exploration of the psyche. The enneagram contains nine 'passions', or organizing principles of the personality: Perfectionist, Giver, Performer, Romantic, Observer, Questioner, Epicure, Boss and Mediator. They are used to characterize parts of the self, which may be dominant or even suppressed. Identifying enneagram types can be used to examine interpersonal relationships and as a tool for understanding oneself and others.

There have been very few nine-fold formations over the years, but those there have been are beautiful, enchanting and inspiring – just like the nine muses of the ancient world.

(RIGHT AND FAR RIGHT) *Cherhill, Wiltshire, England. July 1999. Wheat crop, approximately 200 feet*

CHERHILL, 1999

The beautiful Cherhill nine-fold spinner is another all-time classic crop circle. Nine equilateral triangles and six narrow crescents are combined to create a design of exquisite harmony and proportion.

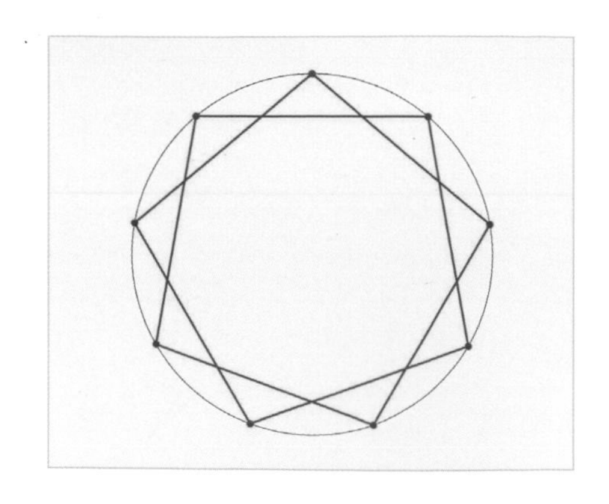

EXPRESSIONS OF NINE

Nine-fold formations are on the whole quite rare. When we reach nine, there are three enneagram stars possible and there is often something quite spectacular about them. Nine, like seven and eleven, always seems to evoke the ineffable when used in design, or in the creation of architectural space. Nine is not easily born from the *vesica*, and yet is the number most associated with birth.

ALDBOURNE, 1999

This formation at Aldbourne was a more traditional nine-pointed star. It occurred during an appalling spell of wet weather and days passed before an aerial record could be made. Since the circle appeared in young barley, the crop began to recover, making the design barely visible. This interesting example illustrates how little crop circles damage the crop in which they appear.

Aldbourne, Wiltshire, England. June 1999. Barley crop, approximately 400 feet

All Cannings, Wiltshire, England. August 2001. Wheat crop, approximately 175 feet

ALL CANNINGS, 2001

The field at All Cannings is close to the Kennett and Avon canal, a major artery that runs through the Pewsey Vale, the location of so many crop circle sites.

This truly beautiful formation is another classic enneagram, perfectly executed. Although a perfect enneagram is impossible to draw, there seems to be no problem with reproducing one here!

Notice the wonderful swirls between each point of the star. Each was unique – various knots and standing twirls of wheat. The centre was a very lovely swirl created by the twisting and splaying of a central tuft of wheat (above right).

Visiting this formation was an absolute pleasure; the atmosphere of the space left a distinct spiritual impression upon the mind.

(ABOVE AND RIGHT) *Woodborough Hill, Wiltshire, England. August 2001. Wheat crop, approximately 200 feet*

WOODBOROUGH HILL, 2001

This formation appeared below Woodborough Hill, a central landmark rising up out of the Pewsey Vale, close to where the Kennett and Avon canal passes by. This amazing circle with its rotational division into nine, had circles locked between arching arms. The crop in which it appeared was long-eared wheat, which has spiny bracts on the seed-heads, and is a lesser-grown crop in the UK.

Ten and Eleven: Transcending the Decad (Part I)

Decagon: Decagram and Hendecagon: Hendecagram

If nine was the culmination of number, the sublime threshold, then ten is the vessel which contains all previous numbers and transports them to a new level, beyond the decad.

As we reach this number, the word 'decad', whilst meaning ten, is also a word for the numbers from one to ten as a whole. This tells us something important; ten is both a number in its own right, and also a collection of numbers; in other words, ten is a new whole. Ten, therefore, is like the monad (one) – but at a different level.

Ten forms the basis of our decimal system, and is also the number of digits on our two hands – fingers and thumbs are very useful when learning to count. Every time we multiply by ten we add a zero, signifying a greater number or level of number. To reach ten is to transcend all that has gone before and reach a new level. Ten-fold geometry is found throughout nature – crabs and lobsters both have ten legs, and citrus fruits often have ten segments.

The first number beyond ten, eleven is yet another that cannot be equally divided to create an equal-sided shape – and approximations have to suffice. Eleven is a very mysterious number, often associated with consciousness and the expansion of consciousness beyond the everyday world. It is the first in what is known as the 'master sequence' of numbers, which unfolds like the eleven times table, 11, 22, 33 and so on.

Eleven is the number which signifies access to other dimensions and governs visionary and mystical states of mind. However, eleven is also mercurial in nature and is also said to be linked with delusion and duplicity.

Eleven is not commonly found in the natural world; it is like those visionary states with which it is associated – elusive and mystical. Like Plato's theory of The Forms, eleven exists only in an ideal state beyond the physical world.

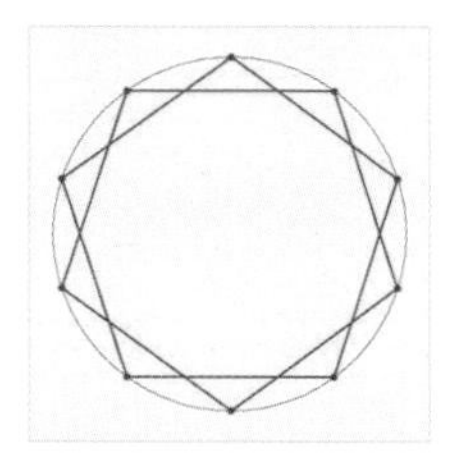

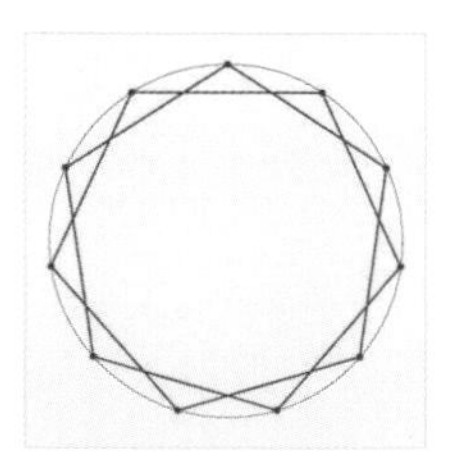
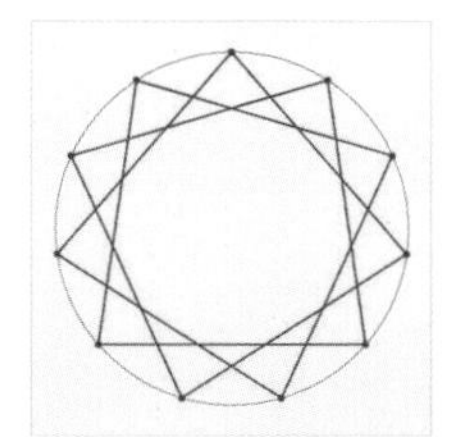
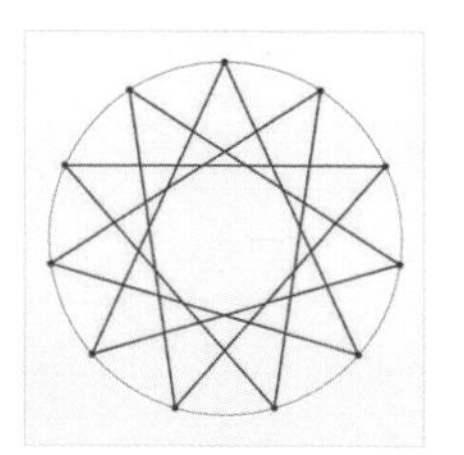
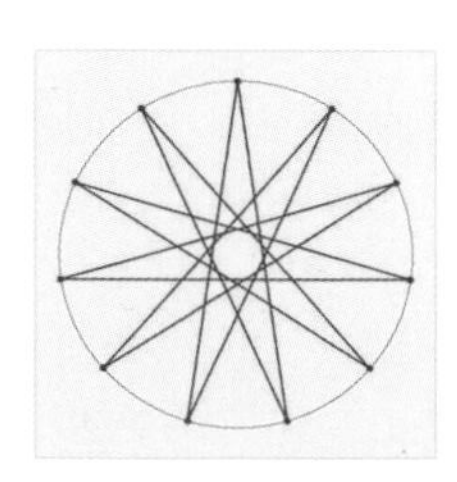

Once we get to a ten-sided shape, seven decagram stars become possible.

(ABOVE AND BELOW) *Martinsell Hill, Wiltshire, England. August 2000. Wheat crop, approximately 200 feet*

MARTINSELL HILL, 2000

This wonderful lotus-like mandala uses ten circles of equal size to define its perimeter, and contains five beautifully-shaped teardrops or petals. The use of ten in any pattern seems to give it a sense of balance and wholeness. The lotus is symbolic of the unfolding of the spirit, and with divine order. Ten is the new unity which holds all the numbers of the decad (from one to nine) and in doing so, takes them onto a new level of function and meaning.

(ABOVE, RIGHT AND ABOVE FAR RIGHT) *Avebury Henge, Wiltshire, England. August 1994. Wheat crop, approximately 250 feet*

AVEBURY HENGE, 1994

Universally know as the 'Avebury Web', this amazing formation was the grand finale of the 1994 crop circle season. The circle is divided into ten equal parts to create the web-like design, with four further horizontal dividers in each section to link the whole pattern together. Interestingly, the centres for the outer circles, which define the undulating pattern of the web, are located beyond the perimeter of the formation itself.

(LEFT AND ABOVE) *Inside the Avebury Web*

NORTH DOWN, 2000

The transcendent North Down formation is the only true eleven-fold formation ever to have appeared. There have been circles that have incorporated eleven components, or numbers that have implied eleven-ness, but geometrically speaking, eleven is incredibly rare. Perhaps this appropriately reflects the rarity of eleven as a number, and its association with transcendental and rarefied visionary states of mind.

The design used curving lines, like folds, to divide the circle into eleven sections. This is difficult enough to approximate on paper, without working on a huge scale. Contemplating the shape, it seems that these curves may suggest a sort of semi-rotational opening and closing of the central space, perhaps a rhythmic gateway of sorts?

Certainly, this formation had a profound effect on many of those that visited it. It seemed to have a unique, almost trance-like atmosphere.

(RIGHT) *North Down, Wiltshire, England. July 2000. Wheat crop, approximately 200 feet*

TWELVE AND THIRTEEN: TRANSCENDING THE DECAD (PART 2)

DODECAGON, DODECAGRAM AND TRISKAIDEKAPHOBIA

The importance of the number twelve can hardly be overstated. Twelve was sometimes known as the solar number that governed the twelve hours of the day and the twelve hours of night and the twelve months of a solar year. Twelve also divided the heavens into the constellations of the zodiac. It was the number used by the ancients as a way to divide time, space and motion. Twelve is the number of the spokes on the great wheel of time, or the wheel of man's fortune.

It was important to some ancient cultures that the Earth should mirror the heavens – 'on Earth as it is in Heaven' – 'as above, so below'. Therefore, the number twelve was enshrined in their units of measurement. The British and US customary 'foot' embodies this idea (there are twelve inches in a foot). Other cultures still use similar twelve-unit systems.

A dodecahedron is a shape with twelve identical faces. Each face is a pentagon, linking the numbers twelve and five together. If five is the number of life, then perhaps twelve is the number of the fulfilment of man's potential. And with this in mind, it is time to meet the last number in our journey – thirteen.

Thirteen is another much maligned number and is often considered unlucky, and to be avoided at all costs. In the Tarot deck, the card bearing this number is called Death – no wonder, then, that it engenders so much fear. Fear of the number thirteen is called 'triskaidekaphobia'.

However, this makes more sense, and becomes a little less doom-laden, when we realize that the number thirteen is the 'number of transformation' – after all, what is death if not the ultimate and most mysterious transformation?

Both twelve and thirteen have been used in crop circle design. Twelves are often beautiful; thirteens, like sevens and elevens, are mysterious and enigmatic.

There are several different twelve-pointed stars possible. If you look closely, this one is in fact made of four equilateral triangles which nicely illustrates the relationship between 3, 4 and 12. The triangles each have three equal sides, multiply them by four and you have the twelve points of the dodecagram.

HONEY STREET, 2001

The amazing Honey Street twelve-fold, repeated the number twelve three times, in each of the three concentric rings. With each successive iteration, the arrow-head shapes become smaller, until finally in the central ring, the arrow-heads become very fine and take on an almost rotational pattern.

Honey Street, Wiltshire, England. August 2001. Wheat crop, approximately 200 feet

EXPRESSIONS OF TWELVE-NESS

For several years a series of bubble-like formations appeared in both Wiltshire and Hampshire, and these incorporated the number twelve. Stephen's Castle Down was a straightforward division by twelve around the perimeter; whereas Bishop's Sutton, whilst still using twelve perimeter circles, has the diameters decreasing and increasing. The Clanfield formation emphasized the relationship between the numbers three and four to twelve-ness (4 x 3 or 3 x 4 = 12).

(ABOVE) *Stephen's Castle Down, Hampshire, England. July 2000. Wheat crop, approximately 200 feet*

(RIGHT) *Clanfield, Hampshire, England. June 1998. Wheat crop, approximately 150 feet*

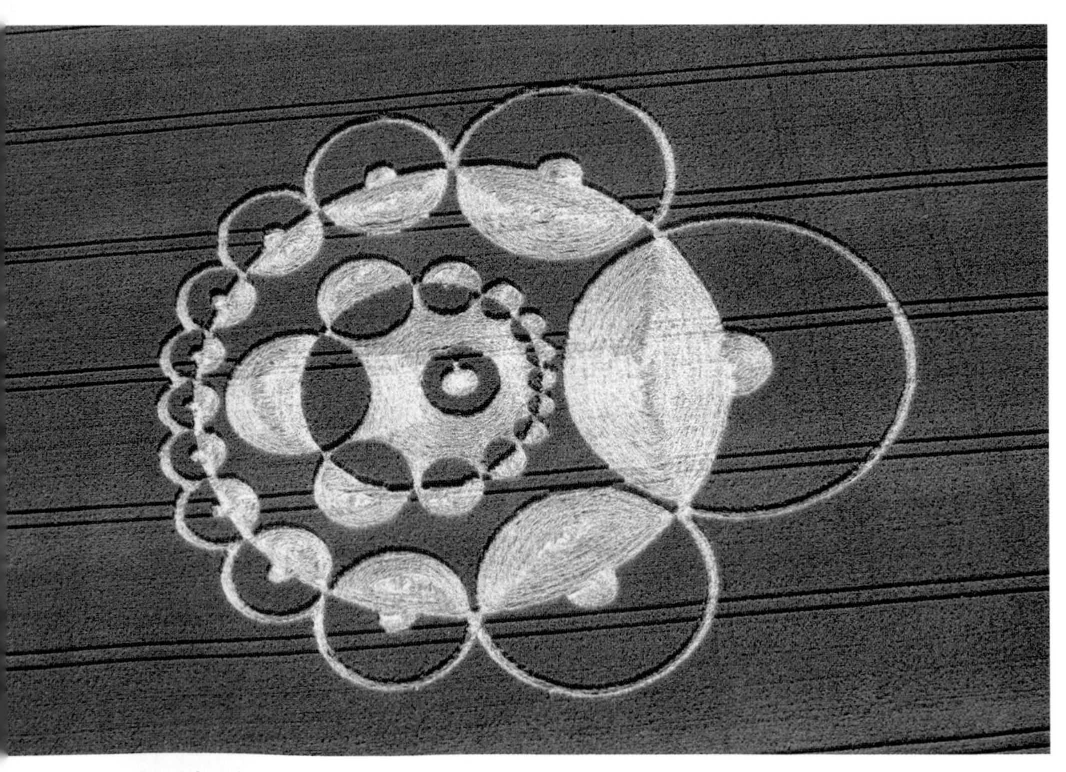

(ABOVE) *Bishop's Sutton, Hampshire, England. July 2000. Wheat crop, approximately 250 feet*

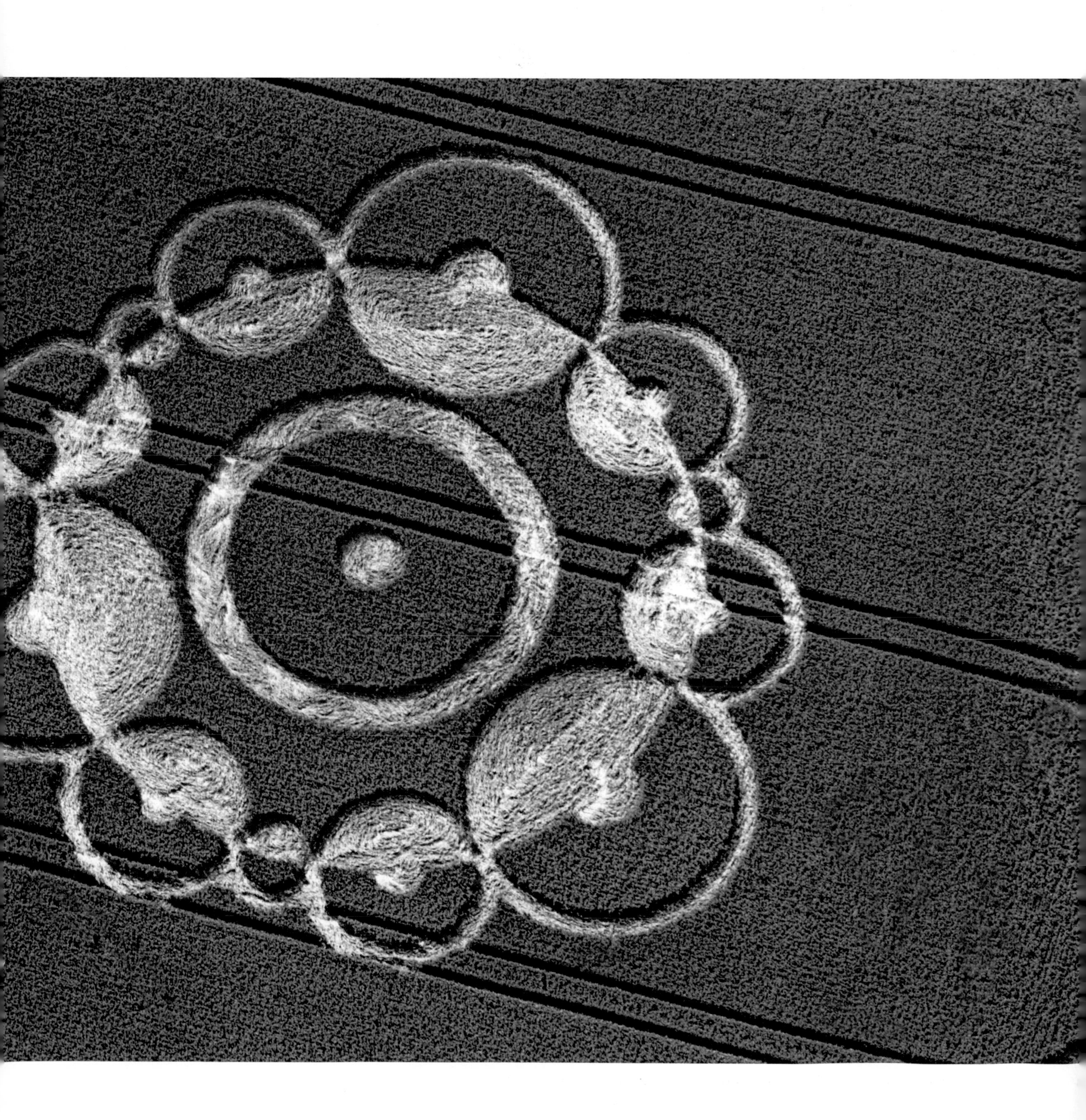

BECKHAMPTON, 2005

Whilst this formation may not appear at first glance to be linked to thirteen, once on the geometer's drawing board, it reveals thirteen centres of curvature required to draw the pattern. This formation measured over one thousand feet in length and was one of the largest formations to appear at that time of year.

(RIGHT) *Beckhampton, Wiltshire, England. June 2005. Barley crop, approximately 1000 feet*

ETCHILHAMPTON, 2004

The interesting formation at Etchilhampton, whilst definitely a thirteen design (thirteen star-points around the outer edge), is simultaneously an eleven and a seven. This formation seems to group together the most mysterious of our numbers and combine them in one design; it is a wonderful geometric accomplishment.

Etchilhampton, Wiltshire, England. July 2004. Wheat crop, approximately 200 feet

Huish, Wiltshire, England. July 2003. Wheat crop, approximately 250 feet

HUISH, 2003

By far the most beautiful authentic thirteen-fold formation was the one that appeared at Huish in 2003. This wonderful thirteen-pointed star was accompanied by thirteen moons and then enclosed in the finest of gossamer rings. This crop circle is a powerful magical talisman of transformation.

CHAPTER TWO

SACRED SPACE

TEMPORARY TEMPLES FOR THE MODERN AGE

Now that we have come to the end of our voyage from one to thirteen, we find that we have the basic vocabulary of the crop circles at our disposal. As you look through the remaining sections of this book, you will be able to spot the basic numbers encoded in the formations to come.

For those with the inclination, drawing the crop circles can be an edifying and insightful undertaking. Black and white silhouettes are often constructed by researchers (with black traditionally denoting the fallen crop) to help search for any hidden (esoteric) geometries underpinning a design. If you follow the crop circles, a medium-sized sketch-book or scrap-book for keeping notes, sketches and cuttings can be invaluable in building up a good picture of any season.

However, before we leave behind the world of geometry there are two further geometric principles that should be discussed when trying to understand the circles. Both are involved specifically in the creation of sacred space and with the ambience created inside the crop circles; one is the squaring of the circle, and the other is the Golden Section.

SQUARING THE CIRCLE

The squaring of the circle is an Ancient Greek geometrical problem or mystical quest. The challenge is to draw both a circle and a square whose perimeters (and areas) are the same, using only a geometer's tools of ruler and compass. Strictly speaking this is an impossible task as the nature of the circle makes it impossible to calculate its precise circumference, which is why we use the never-ending pi. And it is, therefore, clearly impossible to draw a square with an equal measure. However, over time, many close approximations have been discovered (see right for an example), and the squaring of the circle has become a central tenet of sacred geometry to which much special significance has been attached.

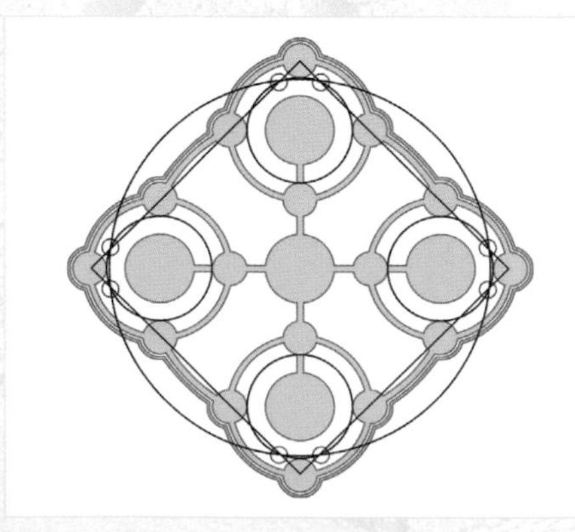

At this juncture, it might be a good question to ask why such an impossible task should be so significant to so many, and should warrant even close approximations so important as to be attempted and devised. When we ask this question we begin to uncover the true significance of this famous geometrical puzzle, because the answer lies in the symbolism of the circle and the square.

As we have already discovered, the unique qualities of the circle are seen to symbolize the Divine, or the divine realm; immeasurable and unknowable. The square is, then, symbolic of the material realm – matter, substance and mass – or in short, the World.

Leonardo da Vinci's famous rendering of Vitruvian Man depicts the squaring of the circle in conjunction with the human form. The drawing explores human proportions in relation to the (divine) circle and the (material) square and perhaps embodies the belief that the human being is partly of the physical world as he has a physical body and partly of the spiritual world as he has an immortal soul. In other words, man himself is a meeting place between heaven and earth.

To ancient temple builders, to the builders of the Gothic cathedrals and other important places of worship, this concept was fundamental. The temple was a meeting place between man and God, between Heaven and Earth. A space that embodied this communion, not only in word and deed but also in stone, would be a space filled with the very essence of this spiritual union. Many temples of antiquity (and some that are standing today) combine the circle and square in their design – the Pantheon, the Al-Aska Mosque and St Peter's Basilica, to name a few.

Many formations have squared the circle but not all are easy to see. Avebury Manor, seen opposite, is one of the best examples.

(ABOVE AND BELOW) *Avebury Manor, Wiltshire, England. July 2005. Approximately 300 feet*

AVEBURY MANOR, 2005

The wonderful Avebury Manor formation of 2005 was the Celtic cross of Celtic crosses. The diagram (left) by the crop circle researcher and geometer Allen Brown shows how the formation squares the circle on a large scale. It does, in fact, square the circle several more times. The design also fits neatly onto a three-by-three (nine) squared grid – which could imply that this is the culmination of the Celtic cross design.

The interior space created by this formation was particularly interesting. It was like walking around a great manor with four wings and many rooms. The centre circle contained a beautiful ring of woven crop, which could be seen even in the aerial photograph. It truly felt like a meeting place of heaven and earth.

THE GOLDEN SECTION

Also called the Golden Proportion, Golden Mean or Golden Ratio, this is one of the most mysterious tenets of Sacred Geometry.

At its most basic, the Golden Section is a way of dividing a line to create a three-fold relationship between the two smaller lines created and the original line before it was divided. The ratio created is 1:0.618... and is better known as 'phi' or ø. Phi is what is called an 'irrational number' – a number that has no whole number resolution and whose decimal places theoretically stretch into infinity; the device phi is used to create the illusion of a whole number, so that it becomes easier to understand and use.

Phi is most commonly associated with the number five, mainly because it is generated over and over again within the geometry of the pentagram. This association is the first clue to some of the deeper and more mysterious aspects of phi, as this ratio lies at the heart of the growth patterns of all living things, including seed germination, root development, leaf distribution and even the dimensions of the human body.

Because of this link, many see the Golden Section as the 'breath of God' as it passes through matter and animates it. Like wave patterns on a beach, the ethereal Golden Section is made visible in growth patterning and shows us where the life-force has acted upon matter.

The Golden Section is also made visible in the spirals of certain shells, pine cones, weather systems and whirlpools; it is the most common spiral found throughout nature. Unlike the Archimedean spiral, whose curves remain constant, the curves of the Golden Spiral increase progressively.

Many artists and philosophers consider the Golden Section as the chief factor in what we consider most beautiful. It has been shown in a number of different ways that human beings have a natural and inbuilt penchant for this ratio – the closer the proportions of the face to that of the Golden Section, the more beautiful we consider it to be.

Both the squaring of the circle and the Golden Section have been used in the creation of sacred space for thousands of years. They are revered for their transcendent effect on human consciousness, for their ability to conjure a symbolic communion between Heaven and Earth and to permeate the subconscious mind with the imprint of sublime beauty and the breath of God, as though breathed into the very space created by these very special proportions and ratios. Their inclusion in crop circle design has lead many to consider the possibility of a mystical or spiritual component to the crop circle mystery.

TEMPORARY TEMPLES FOR THE MODERN AGE

If you have ever visited a truly great temple or cathedral, you may well have been moved by its architectural space. Many of the great buildings of antiquity were designed using nature's canon of number and proportion – exactly the same canon of number and proportion we find in the crop circles. Specifically, architects used the marriage of the circle and square to symbolize the temple or church as a meeting place between man and God, and the Golden Section represents the ineffable power of God to breath life into the world.

Crop circles can have a very similar, if not parallel, effect to that of temples or cathedrals, and it is interesting to notice the way people behave inside the formations. Although their size regularly prevents much understanding of their overall shape at ground-level, the effect of their spaces on visitors is often remarkable. Some of the larger

Harmonic forms in water under the effect of sound vibrations. These standing wave patterns occur within small samples of water placed upon a lens and illuminated from below, while vibrating in response to specific audible frequencies (Cymatics)

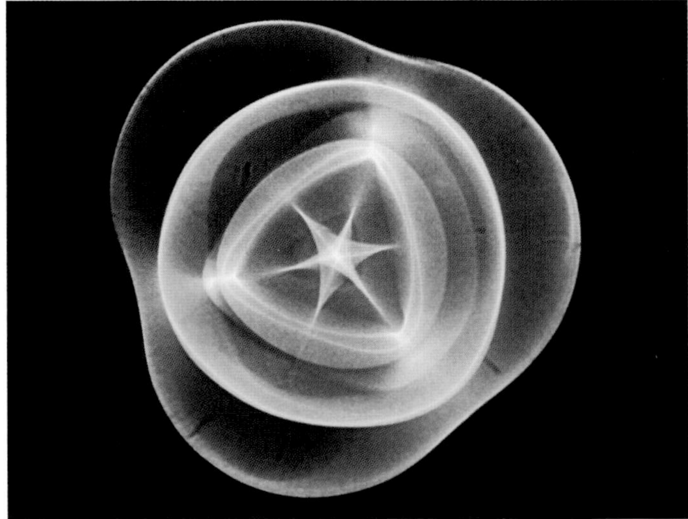

PEWSEY WHITE HORSE, 2002

During the summer of 2002, this wonderful shell-like formation appeared. It was immediately nicknamed the Nautilus Shell. The nautilus is noted for its Golden Section spiral shape. Both the shell and this formation embody the proportions of growth found throughout all living organisms. The human ear is based upon the same spiral, including the delicate inner section known as the cochlea, which receives vibrations from the outside world. The human embryo also develops in the same shape. The wonderful thing about this spiral is that it unfolds from within itself, a curious property, which means that in a way it makes visible the invisible, creating something from seemingly nothing. Another fascinating property is that as it unfolds, its numbers reach towards a resolution of the ineffable phi, becoming ever closer but never reaching its goal.

Pewsey, Wiltshire, England. July 2002. Wheat crop, approximately 200 feet

circles, in particular, are awe-inspiring in their size and construction. Inside the formations, the water-like flow of the laid crop, upon which you walk, gives a sense of movement, and the summer sunshine reflects off its surface, changing as you move around. Visitors become calm and seek out a quiet spot to sit and contemplate their experience. Often people feel drawn towards the centre of the formation, or some other significant point. This kind of experience has become commonplace in crop circle lore but why should this be?

The answer seems to lie with the crop circles' shapes; but why the circle, why the triangle, why the square?

Shape is a fundamental response to vibration. There is a science of vibration; it is called Cymatics and was formally invented and named in the 1950s by Hans Jenny, a Swiss scientist. By linking vibrating plates to amplifiers and oscilloscopes to monitor and change the frequency of the vibration being applied, Jenny was able to show that matter responds directly to vibration, by ordering itself according to the frequency used. Jenny applied vibrations to many different materials, for example, oil of turpentine floating on water; and volumes of liquid, for example, from tanks of water to small drops of it on a lens. When these water drops are lit from below (see left), the resulting patterns from vibrations acting on the water can be seen and photographed. The results are surprisingly geometric and many look very much like crop circle patterns, leading people to speculate that vibration might be involved in crop circles' creation.

Now consider the fact that sounds and music are also vibrations. They are vibrations of a frequency that are audible to the human ear; there are of course many frequencies, both low and high, that we cannot hear.

We know that sounds, and especially music, can have a profound psychological effect upon us. Music can move us to tears, terrify us, and evoke a wide range of other emotions. If shape is a fundamental response to vibration, it stands to reason that shape may have a similar effect on the psyche. Although inaudible and at present unmeasurable, it has been postulated that we might be sensitive to such a subtle phenomenon as this, and that it may have a distinct psychological effect similar to that evoked by music.

Many believe that some of the ancients were well aware of this kind of phenomenon and used it deliberately to great effect in the temples of antiquity. Crop circles could therefore be regarded as 'Temporary Temples for the Modern Age': although only transitory (due to being formed in crops), whilst in situ they create a space which engenders a sense of power and sacredness that is undeniably palpable.

CHAPTER THREE

LABYRINTHS, MAZES AND PUZZLES

LOST AND FOUND

I wonder if you have ever felt as if you were utterly lost; the way forward seems full of false dawns and dead ends? Or perhaps you have felt that there was something missing, some elusive piece that if you could just find (or even turn around) would make things complete? Or maybe at times you have felt that no matter what you do, your life seems determined to follow some mysterious pre-ordained path? If so, you are already intimately acquainted with the archetypal world of labyrinths, mazes and puzzles.

Almost since the inception of civilization, labyrinths, mazes and puzzles have been used as metaphors for the journey or pattern of life. It is in our very nature to seek out patterns, connect the dots, it is these vital skills that help us recognize things and ultimately to make sense of our life. It is another example of how important the idea of shape and pattern is to our minds.

Before we go any further, a couple of definitions would be helpful. Labyrinths and mazes are not the same and they are often confused. A labyrinth is a single winding pathway, which one can but follow; whereas a maze offers a choice of pathways, in which you can get lost. The labyrinth is ritually walked, with several preordained curves, which lead inexorably to the centre – no other route is offered or is possible. The traditional labyrinth has between five and eight turns, the one in Chartres cathedral has thirteen. Once again, the numbers at play can reveal much about the principle behind each design; thirteen is the number of transformation, the goal of the Chartres labyrinth and of the Christian belief in life beyond death for the faithful. The labyrinth may also be symbolic of the self, at its centre the heart or essence of the self. The purpose of life is to find that authentic self, to strip away the layers and masks (symbolized by the turns) and to find our true nature. In contrast, the maze is about choice and consequence. A maze offers many pathway choices, but only the right one will get you to the centre and back again; the wrong choice will see you helplessly lost. Puzzles are about choice too, but they are about challenges and resolutions. The key to many puzzles is imagination and the ability to see things from a different perspective.

In the world of labyrinths, mazes and puzzles, you can lose yourself hopelessly, or maybe find your true and unfettered self.

WEST KENNETT, 2004

This wonderful eight-sided star (octogram) contained an inner circle divided into four. Each quadrant contained a labyrinthine spiral, which curved around into the centre, following the quarter shape of the section. However, interestingly, the entrance to each section appears unclear. Four-ness seems to pervade this design, although the outer perimeter looks like an octogram, it could also be seen as two overlaid squares, with the four inner sections also speaking of four.

West Kennett, Wiltshire, England. July 2004.
Wheat crop, approximately 300 feet

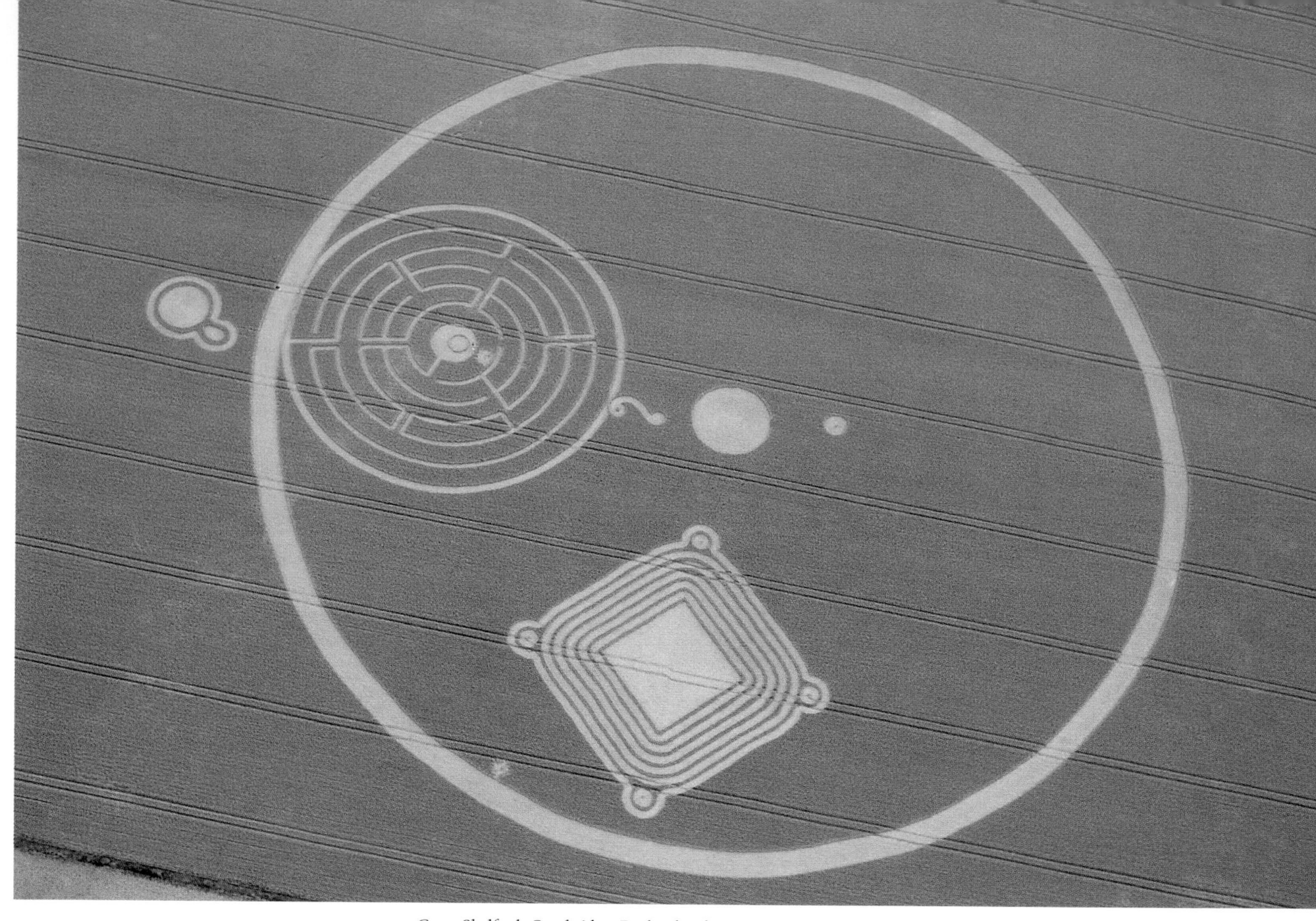

Great Shelford, Cambridge, England. July 2001. Wheat crop, approximately 600 feet

THE QUATERNITY OF THE SELF

The question of the mandala is something we will consider further in later pages, but if labyrinths and mazes can be seen as symbolic of the self, then this four-fold design surely represents what Jung called 'The Quaternity of the Self'. Jung believed that there were four basic functions of the self – thinking, feeling, sensing and intuition – and that these functions were the basis of our interaction with the world. The intersection on the circle with two lines at right-angles to one other seems instinctual and natural. This labyrinthine formation seemed to be an invitation to walk each quadrant considering our four-fold self; which is our most dominant sense and which is our most underdeveloped?

GREAT SHELFORD, 2001

This astonishing formation is one of the largest crop circle rings on record. The maze itself was 237 feet in diameter; still it looks dwarfed by its giant enclosing circle, which had a diameter of 666 feet. This is a real maze and there is a real solution, can you find it?

Even though this formation seems to have no overall organization or order, there is some lovely detail work. The tiny scroll attached to the maze is just beautiful. And the group of six nested squares, seven with curved corners, is also very pleasing to the eye; the spacing between each square is wonderfully regular.

The maze can also be likened to the spider's web. Folklore tells us that the maze was used to temporarily entrap unwanted or troublesome spirits. Once led into the maze, these bothersome entities would have to remain there until they managed to find their way out – thus ensuring a period of relief for those unfortunate enough to have attracted their attentions.

In other tales, it is the spirits that dwell in the maze. The fate of those who stray within their realm is perpetual bewilderment and eternal wandering.

Far from being a puzzle of pure reason and logic, the maze is also a mystical space that carries a fascinating warning about enchantment and entrapment.

West Woods, Lockeridge, Wiltshire. June 2005. Wheat crop, approximately 200 feet

WEST WOODS, LOCKERIDGE, 2005

This formation is based upon a spiral made from box shapes, gradually increasing in size from the centre. The central spiral shape is then enclosed by eight further boxes with strangely curved ends. The whole design is then placed within a containing circle.

The link between the labyrinth and the spiral lies in the fact that to walk a spiral is like walking a labyrinth. We move from the outer regions progressively into the centre.

The whole point of the labyrinth is to reach the centre and many crop circle designs are labyrinthine in nature; they encourage or invite a journey to be made to the heart of the formation. Some are more obvious than others, but many who visited this lovely formation at West Woods instinctively felt the need ritually to walk the inner spiral to reach the centre.

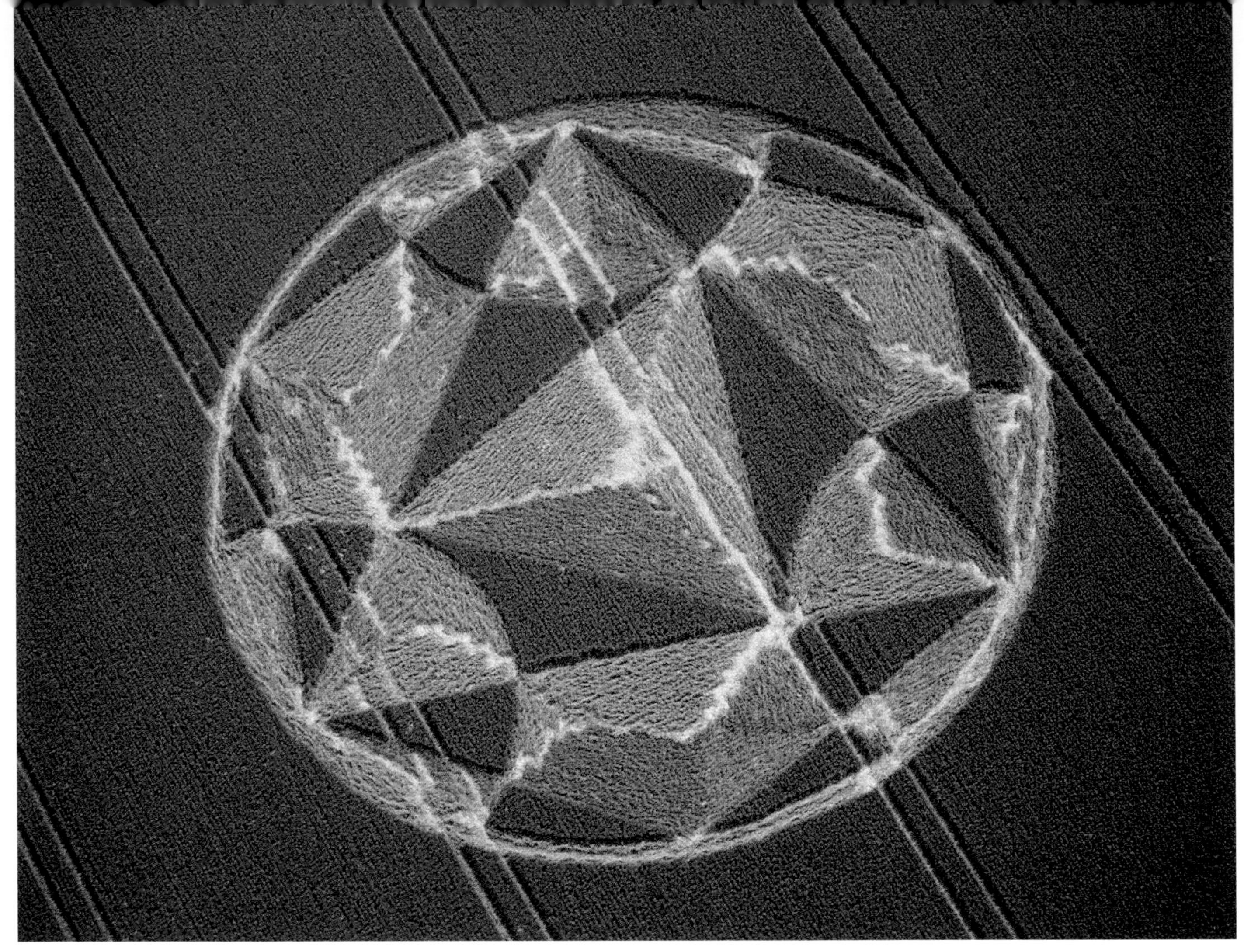

(Above and below) *Bishops Cannings Down, Wiltshire, England. June 2000. Wheat crop, approximately 150 feet*

Bishops Cannings Down, 2000

The formation above was a real puzzle of standing and fallen shapes which when pieced together form a circle. It was quickly nicknamed the 'Chinese Puzzle' in reference to its puzzling nature.

WADEN HILL, 2005

This lovely formation has a puzzling centre. The central triangle presents us with an optical illusion, a three-dimensional shape which cannot exist in three-dimensional space. Over the years, crop circles have presented us with a number of optical illusions which seem to defy our reality constructs.

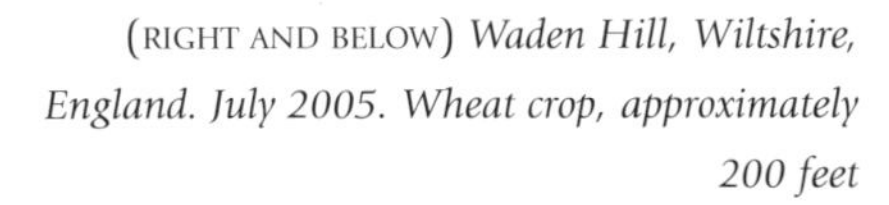

(RIGHT AND BELOW) *Waden Hill, Wiltshire, England. July 2005. Wheat crop, approximately 200 feet*

Aldbourne, Wiltshire, England. August 2004. Wheat crop, approximately 300 feet

ALDBOURNE, 2004

This amazing formation at Aldbourne was something of a puzzle. The interior pattern is overlaid onto a nine-by-nine grid and contains sixty-nine squares of varied design, with three squares on each corner seemingly missing. At first this might not seem important, but it is in fact a clue to the hidden geometry that underpins this design. Imagine that a circle is drawn around the inner grid, clipping the corners of the grid design where squares appear to be missing. Then we square the design by drawing a square around the grid. This circle and square are in a squared circle relationship (in area), accurate to about 97.5 percent.

The designs of the individual squares are also intriguing. Some are just standing squares, whilst others are combinations of standing and flattened squares; each square is further divided into four to allow this patterning. Many numbers are at play, but the numbers four and nine seem most prevalent.

The pattern seems to show a huge X or cross at its centre and its meaning is a mystery. I have often wondered if it refers to the idea of multiplication, the key to unlocking the area of any shape; in this case, the areas of the circle and square and the squared circle relationship between the two.

FOREST HILL, NEAR SAVERNAKE, 2004

This huge circle at Savernake was based on a nine square grid. If you turn alternate squares another pattern is formed. There are three different possibilities of design for this circle, depending on the rotation of the nine squares.

(LEFT) *Savernake Forest, Wiltshire, England. July 2004. Wheat crop, approximately 300 feet*

BECKHAMPTON, 1995

This circle could easily have been included in our section on spirals; however, such was the effect of the interior on those that visited it, that almost everyone felt under obligation to walk it and follow its meanderings, around and around, into the centre and then out again. The labyrinthine intent of this design was unmistakable, and utterly compelling.

This spiral contained nine revolutions, which had to be negotiated before reaching the centre – nine steps, phases or stages to be navigated and passed through in order to find the heart or essence of this design.

Nine is the number of culmination, which contains all before it and which resides at the threshold of basic number. There seemed to be something portentous and potentially transformative about the numbers encoded in this design.

(LEFT, ABOVE AND RIGHT)
Beckhampton, Wiltshire, England. May 1995. Barley crop, approximately 200 feet

CHAPTER FOUR

KNOTS, ROPES AND RIBBONS

THE TIES THAT BIND US TOGETHER

Rope, thread, ribbon: they are all intimately connected with *measure*. They can be used to establish and replicate distances accurately. Rope or thread can assist in the demarcation of any space and, before the geometer's compass, the rope and marker were the basic apparatus needed for the creation of a circle. The simplest compass can be made from a pencil and a length of thread; by anchoring one end of the thread with a finger or a pin and tying the pencil to the other end, a circle may be drawn by circling the pencil around the secure centre point – keeping the thread taut.

When a thread or rope is tied with knots at regular intervals it can then be used to create other important shapes, including the right-angled triangle (90 degrees) and other angles and forms necessary for construction and building. A rope with 13 equally spaced knots can help create a whole series of fundamental shapes without the need for a ruler, or even a grasp of basic geometry.

Symbolically the rope, thread or ribbon is a tether; perhaps a link or ladder between Heaven and Earth; it represents that intimate connection between mother and child, the umbilical cord; the rope, thread and cord imply connection, relationship, binding and eternal love.

Knots signify the binding together of two or more parts, the lovers' knot signifies the entwining of hearts and bodies in the mystical act of love – the never-ending knot is a symbol of eternity. However, some knots signify bondage when they are used to constrain or restrict freedom. They can also symbolise confusion, disorder, irresolvable chaos and even madness.

Of course, one cannot talk about threads and knots without mentioning weaving. Weaving is an ancient craft, which is also symbolic of connection, relationship, shape and pattern. Gold and silver threads and ribbons of all colours have been used in the art of decoration for thousands of years. Often they are used to draw attention to important people, or perhaps a beautiful face. The belt or sash is a common symbol of authority or rank.

How often do we hear people describe themselves as being 'tied up in knots' or 'tied down', feeling 'duty bound'; in psychology they speak of 'the ties that bind'. Knots, ropes and ribbons are an integral part of our lives and our way of thinking; they are another archetypal theme that literally binds humanity together.

WINDMILL HILL, 2003

This formation at Windmill Hill clearly represents rope or twisted thread. It contains twelve segments that lock together. The shape is four-sided, combining the idea of the square and the rope. If four represents material reality and the world, and twelve represents the destiny of man, then perhaps this cord represents man's fate of being temporarily tethered to this earthly realm.

Windmill Hill, Wiltshire, England. June 2003. Barley crop, approximately 300 feet

Beckhampton, Wiltshire, England. July 1999. Wheat crop, approximately 200 feet

BECKHAMPTON, 1999

This design mimics a folded and flattened ribbon. The ribbon is folded into a knot with no beginning or end; two triangular shapes are combined to create a six-fold form. The elegance of this design is easy to overlook, and the ingenious layout ensures that the central space remains open and accessible to visitors via the folds in the ribbon, which are outlined by narrow tracks. The central element seems to imply some sort of movement, almost like the shutter mechanism of a camera, which would open and close with a rotational movement.

ADAMS GRAVE, 2000

The lovely basket-weave circle below Adams Grave (an ancient longbarrow) is one of only a small number to have their floor patterns woven in such a specialized manner. Walking on top of this carpet of wheat was rather disconcerting, as you were painfully aware of the damage you were causing!

Weaving is one of the oldest craft forms known to man and often involves rhythmic, iterative movement and patterning, another important principle found in nature.

Etchilhampton, 2002

The huge ribbon-esque formation at Etchilhampton measured approximately 300 feet in diameter. This was yet another six-fold design, with six inter-connected circles or loops of ribbon. Once again, access was gained via the folds of the ribbons. Interestingly, the central space was implied rather than actual, it was the meeting point or mysterious emanating point for the ribbon itself.

(RIGHT) *Etchilhampton, Wiltshire, England. August 2002. Wheat crop, approximately 400 feet*

(BELOW) *Adam's Grave, Alton Barnes, Wiltshire, England. July 2000. Wheat crop, approximately 120 feet*

AVEBURY TRUSLOE, 2002

The year 2002 was a year of ribbons, knots and ropes; the theme was explored many times that summer. One of the first circles to appear was the lovely Celtic knot at Avebury Trusloe. The formation used more six-fold geometry in its design; in fact many of the ribbon formations seem concerned with six-ness, order and structure in space. Once again, this was a never-ending knot, six overlapping loops confined within an implied circle. Curiously, there were thirty-nine tiny loops around the perimeter of this circle, rather irregularly placed, thirty-nine divided by three is thirteen, the transformative number.

Avebury Trusloe, Wiltshire, England. June 2002. Barley crop, approximately 200 feet

Stonehenge, Wiltshire, England. July 2002. Wheat crop, approximately 750 feet

STONEHENGE, 2002

It is always considered a rare and marvellous privilege when a crop circle occurs close to Stonehenge, one of England's most famous ancient sites. The circles are interpreted as important formations and often attract the media and a wider public attention. This fantastic example appeared in July 2002, early in the season and not reserved for a spectacular grand finale in August, as one might expect. There were several noteworthy things about this formation that we should take time to consider. First is its immense size; at approximately 750 feet in diameter, this design was an excellent example of the relationship between size and power. Second is the way this circle was positioned in the field, which contained a number of round barrows (ancient burial mounds). Note how several of the arms clip one or more of these barrows or, as in one case, the perimeter of the field. This gives the impression of the formation being nestled between these features. Its placement implies considerable skill working on a large scale. This circle, like so many others, appeared in its entirety overnight, complete, whole and perfect; stretching the imagination considerably as to its possible origins.

Once more, six-fold geometry is embodied in this design with six billowing ribbons emanating from a mysterious empty space in the centre. Close to the centre, the pattern hints at a rose-type design, but a rotational unfolding also appears to be suggested (as with several of the ribbon formations). The underpinning geometry is entirely circular, meaning that the whole design can be picked from a series of underlying circles.

There is something in this shape that speaks of freedom and generation. This formation seems to be a frozen snapshot of movement in space, of free-flowing, unbound liberty. Perhaps this idea was also echoed in the date of the formation: 4 July, American Independence Day.

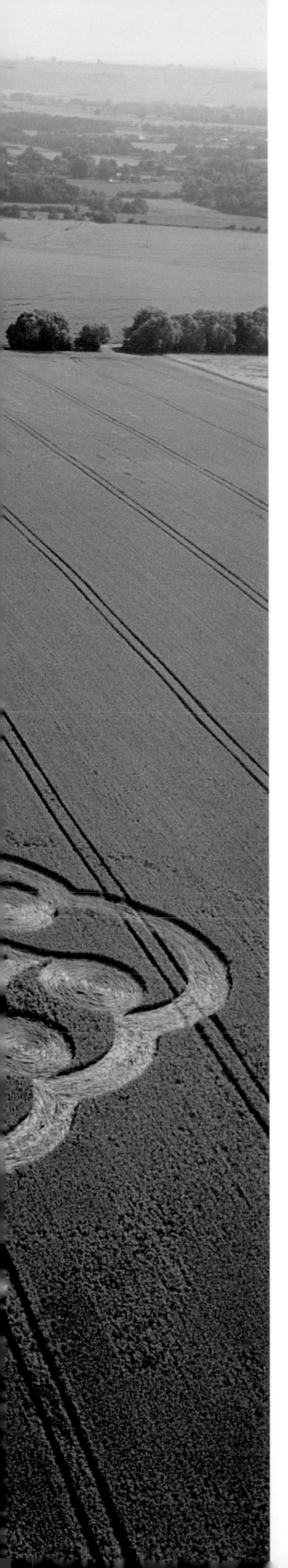

(LEFT AND ABOVE) *South Field, Alton Barnes, Wiltshire, England. August 2003. Wheat crop, approximately 300 feet*

SOUTH FIELD, 2003

South Field 2003, was the second of this pair to appear. Its outer square could quite conceivably be either a knotted rope or chain with many links. Each of the perimeter circles had beautifully swirled and knotted centres, while the exquisite centre used eight-fold geometry to create a spiralling star-like design.

SOUTH FIELD, 2002

The sublime beauty of the South Field 2002 formation is difficult to deny. Three diminishing square-shaped ropes are contained within a circle on top of a natural rise. Perhaps this speaks of our inexorable tether to material reality or perhaps those who stood inside this incredible formation would say that this play on the circle and square was a temporary meeting place of Heaven and Earth, and a representation of the mystical tie that connects the two.

(ABOVE AND RIGHT)
South Field, Alton Barnes, Wiltshire, England. July 2002. Wheat crop, approximately 300 feet

CHAPTER FIVE

SPIRALS AND SPINNERS

SPINNING INTO ECSTASY

Everyone has had their head in a spin over one thing or another. Spinning can be a metaphor for disorientation, confusion, even delirium; it can signify feeling out of control.

Sufis have been spinning and whirling themselves into states of ecstasy for thousands of years. During their dervish dances they deliberately disorientate their conscious minds, to gain access to altered states of consciousness.

Above all, spirals and spinners are about movement, unfolding and growth. Nature often uses unfolding in her growth processes; the unfurling of spirals in ferns, petals and the human foetus are just a few examples of how fundamental this principle is to the world in which we live. We are, in fact, in a constant state of spinning and revolving. Our planet rotates on its axis once every twenty-four hours and orbits around the sun once every year. On a larger scale, our whole galaxy is spinning, and even though we might feel as if we are standing perfectly still, we are actually moving at an incredible speed through space.

Foucault's Pendulum demonstrates the movement of the earth, and the universe beyond, around the dimensionless still centre round which the whole of creation moves. The pendulum can be made to mark its path by tracing lines and curves onto sand; theoretically, the end of the pattern should meet up perfectly with the beginning, if the pendulum has been placed exactly on one of the earth's two poles. This neatly illustrates how fundamental spinning, swirling and unfolding are to the nature of life on Earth and the universe. The patterns traced by these pendulums are often similar to crop circle designs.

Other familiar spirals include swirling weather systems. Hurricanes, typhoons, tornados and whirlwinds are fundamentally spiralling weather patterns – the larger weather systems are beautiful when seen from space, although sometimes deadly when encountered on Earth. Spirals and spinning occur when two opposing forces meet and they move around each other, trying to find a resolution. Spirals are intimately connected with gravity, which tempers their speed, direction and size.

Spirals and spinners are an integral part of the crop circle phenomenon, the circle floor-lays often display evidence of a revolving force moving over and through the crop, leaving in its wake exquisite swirled carpets of wheat and barley stems. Often, crop circle designs incorporate a sense of spinning movement in their shapes.

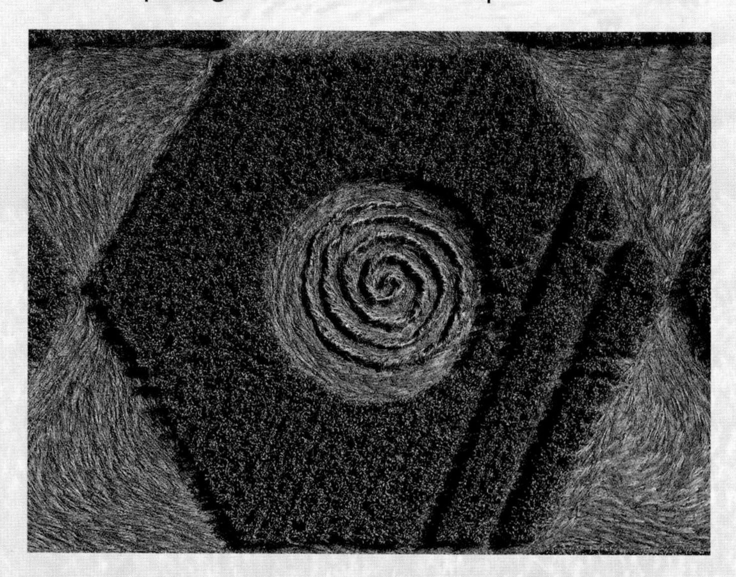

WILTON WINDMILL, 2004

This lovely formation close to the Wilton Windmill could easily have been a blueprint for a six-fold set of windmill sails. In the centre, a tiny and exquisite spiral of weaved crop appeared as if indicating the direction of rotation for the new set of sails.

Wilton Windmill, Wiltshire, England. August 2004. Wheat crop, approximately 250 feet

PORTSDOWN HILL, 2004

The double spiral at Portsdown Hill was a pair of wonderfully realized Archimedean spirals. Archimedean spirals work like the rolling up of a tape measure, a continuous, spiral shape that increases in size only enough to accommodate the next turn.

(RIGHT) Portsdown Hill, Hampshire, England. June 2004. Barley crop, approximately 200 feet

(LEFT) Knoll Down, Wiltshire, England. July 2002. Wheat crop, approximately 300 feet

KNOLL DOWN, 2002

The enormous formation at Knoll Down looked like a huge Ferris wheel. The circle was divided into seventy-six equal segments. Seven and six equal thirteen, the number of transformation. Here spinning is used as a metaphor for transformation.

WEST OVERTON, 2002

This double spiral looks like two coiled serpents. But there is a subtle visual illusion here – follow the flattened heads of the serpents into the centre of the formation and you will notice they do not match up with their standing tails!

West Overton, Wiltshire, England. June 2002. Barley crop, approximately 250 feet

Dunley, Hampshire, England. July 2003. Linseed crop, approximately 50 feet

DUNLEY, 2003

This small but gorgeous circle appeared in linseed crop. The tiny blue flowers make this a stunning canvas for the crop circles. At the centre of the pattern there is another spiral shape: the whole design seems to have an American Indian feel to it.

The Sanctuary, Wiltshire, England. August 2002. Wheat crop, approximately 200 feet

THE SANCTUARY, 2002

The double spiral at The Sanctuary presented two opposing spirals joined at the centre and enclosed within a containing circle. It looked like a lovely form of scroll work.

HONEY STREET, 2004

The stunning six-armed star at Honey Street was a lovely piece of design. The arms (reminiscent of the ribbon formations) seemed to float about the central circle, spinning like a child's windmill toy in the breeze.

Honey Street, Alton Barnes, Wiltshire. June 2004. Wheat crop, approximately 200 feet

Windmill Hill, Wiltshire, England. June 2003. Barley crop, approximately 200 feet

WINDMILL HILL, 2003

The circle at Windmill Hill was a five-fold spinner, consisting of five crescent moon-shapes all nested together. Flying around these spinning designs from the air reveals their sense of movement and rotation. These circles take on a whole new aura once seen in motion from the air.

HACKPEN HILL, 1999

The spiralling Hackpen Hill circle mixed circular and triangular geometry to create a wonderful rose-like design. You could not walk inside the three fine lines at the perimeter, they were just too narrow.

Hackpen Hill, Wiltshire, England. July 1999. Wheat crop, approximately 400 feet

THE SANCTUARY, 1998 AND KINGSCLERE, 1995

Here are two more spinners; the movement was palpable from within the formations on the ground. The star- or saw-like arms of each seemed to swish and whoosh around the interior of the formation, just above the flattened crop. Perhaps the crop circles themselves revolve and unfold as they appear; everything about these designs suggests that they might.

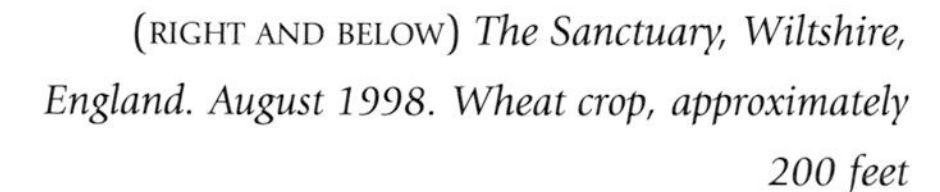

(RIGHT AND BELOW) *The Sanctuary, Wiltshire, England. August 1998. Wheat crop, approximately 200 feet*

(RIGHT AND BELOW) *Watership Down, Kingsclere, Hampshire, England. July 1995. Wheat crop, approximately 150 feet*

CHAPTER SIX

FORMS OF LIFE

ALL CREATURES GREAT AND SMALL

Some of the most bizarre and difficult crop circles to interpret have been those that take the form of living creatures. Whilst some crop formations clearly depict life-forms with which we are familiar, some have presented us with visions of the alien and unknown. How are we to approach these creatures? What are we to make of them?

Animals, creatures, monsters and mythical beasts are a fundamental part of our real and imaginary lives and their forms are indelibly and deeply etched into the human psyche. Our connection with animals is emphasized by our keeping of family pets, the farming of animals, and the array of creatures we keep in captivity in zoos and amusement parks.

However, nowhere is the animal form more at work than in our dreams, nightmares, legends and nowadays, in the world of cinema – just think of the adrenalin-inducing Jaws, Godzilla or King Kong. For many of us, there is nothing more terrifying than a monster, a giant spider or a snake. In some ways animals can represent our own animal nature; as the pre-eminent animal on the planet, it is perhaps only when we meet the monstrous that we come face-to-face with our own limitations and fragility.

Our earliest ancestors included numerous animals in their cave paintings, even creatures that combined both animal and man (therianthropes). Great cultures have also venerated deities that either combine human and animal forms or actually take on animal shapes. Animals can embody noble qualities or become synonymous with them; like the cunning fox, the wise owl and the faithful dog. The Great Bear, Taurus the Bull and Cancer the Crab, along with many others, are creatures that have been elevated to the heavens as star constellations in our night sky. With the incredible diversity of life on this planet, who can say what other forms of life might exist elsewhere – perhaps the crop circles offer us the opportunity to consider this very question along with that of our own animal nature.

Beckhampton, Wiltshire, England. July 1998. Wheat crop, approximately 350 feet

BECKHAMPTON, 1998

The huge Beckhampton formation had a definite aquatic feel to it and was quickly named the Manta Ray. Its extremely long tail was made from a succession of tiny circles and ended with a grouping that looked like some kind of stinger. The interior space of the body contained a remarkable floor-lay, with the crop swept in all directions. It was not until we saw the aerial view that the patterning made any sense.

Tan Hill, Alton Barnes, Wiltshire, England. July 2004. Wheat crop, approximately 350 feet

TAN HILL, 2004

This amazing crop circle was formed over four consecutive nights, an unusual, if not unprecedented, event. There is a sense of both beauty and grace in its appearance, which uses the ever-decreasing circles template to create a tail and the wings (or arms).

(ABOVE AND BELOW) *Bishops Cannings, Wiltshire, England. July 1994. Wheat crop, approximately 500 feet*

BISHOPS CANNINGS, 1994

The Bishops Cannings Scorpion was one of the most spectacular crop circles to appear during 1994. Placed in a sloping field by a main road, its enormous form was visible to thousands of passers-by. The design was based on circular components and its tail contained eleven circles decreasing in size, making the length of the creature simply huge. Inside its great body, the formation was beautifully laid and swirled, the boundary edges of each component were crisp and precise.

WINDMILL HILL, 2004 AND WILSFORD, 1994

The Windmill Hill formation seemed to float just above the crop as if suspended in water or in the air. Was this a biological form or a mechanical one? Whatever it was, visitors to this circle experienced a whole range of electrical faults to their cameras and mobile phones whilst inside it. The formation at Wilsford, although probably not a creature itself, is of the same type. Nicknamed the Thought Bubble, many circle designs have occurred using a succession of increasing or decreasing circles; many have also been creature-like.

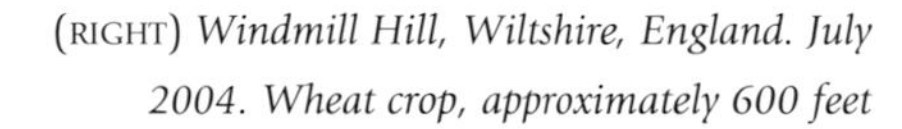

(RIGHT) *Windmill Hill, Wiltshire, England. July 2004. Wheat crop, approximately 600 feet*

Wilsford, Wiltshire, England. July 1994. Wheat crop, approximately 400 feet

GOLDEN BALL HILL, 2004 AND ALTON BARNES, 2002

Dolphins have been a theme for the crop circle phenomenon on several occasions. Here are two formations that seem to show pairs of dolphins or dolphin twins. As one of the earth's most intelligent animal species, it is interesting that they are depicted. Whilst these images may seem contrived, these designs are created using the same canon of shape and proportion from which all other circles are made. With environmental pollution and animal extinctions on the rise, one ponders the significance of these kinds of designs.

(LEFT) *Golden Ball Hill, Wiltshire, England. July 2004. Wheat crop, approximately 300 feet*

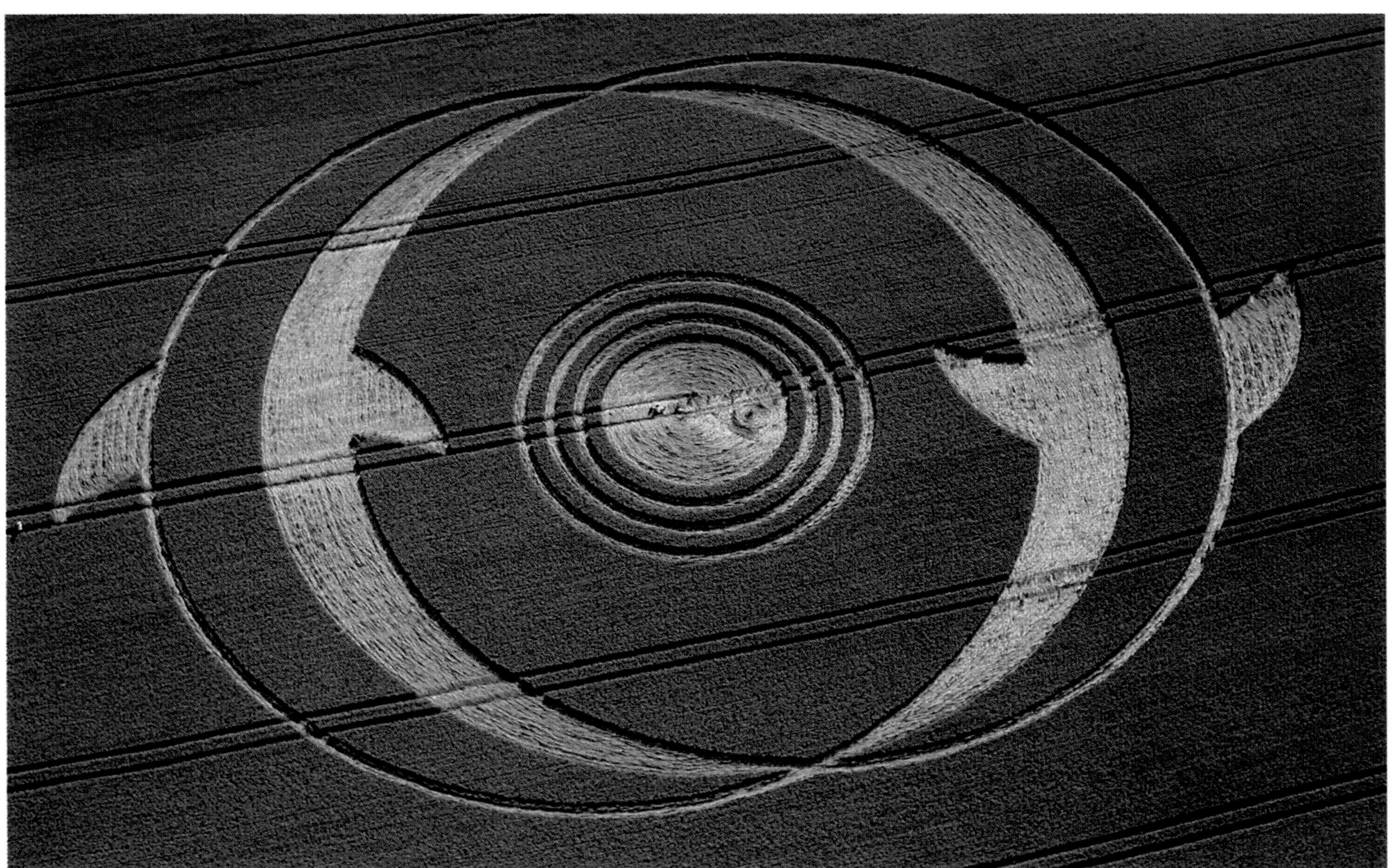

East Field, Alton Barnes, Wiltshire, England. August 2002. Wheat crop, approximately 250 feet

BARBURY CASTLE, 1999 AND ALTON BARNES, 2005

Three interlocking crescents inside a narrow standing ring are then encased in a further flattened circle. Is this formation three more dolphins or is it a design of bananas? The way the crescent shapes intertwine is absolutely beautiful. Notice how one end of each crescent, as it crosses another, gives each 'dolphin' a fin? The scarab at Alton Barnes had its wings open and seemed to be carrying a sun-disc. The scarab was sacred to the Ancient Egyptians and was associated with rebirth and transformation.

(RIGHT) *Barbury Castle, Wiltshire, England. July 1999. Wheat crop, approximately 200 feet*

East Field, Alton Barnes, Wiltshire, England. August 2005. Wheat crop, approximately 100 feet

WOODBOROUGH HILL, NEAR ALTON BARNES, 2003

This combination of bird and serpent was located beneath Woodborough Hill, a focus for strange and inexplicable sightings of light phenomena and other ghostly occurrences. It is reminiscent of the feathered serpent, Quetzalcoatl, venerated by the Aztecs (and known to the Maya as Kukulcan) although admittedly they never represented him like this in their art works. The mixing of bird and serpent species seems uniquely and essentially Meso-American. In some traditions, Quetzalcoatl was a civilizing god who, for a while, turned the people away from their human sacrifices and encouraged them to create a more cultured society. Other legends tell us that he came from a race of god-like men, from a civilization destroyed by cataclysm whose survivors had been scattered all over the face of the earth.

Woodborough Hill, Alton Barnes, Wiltshire, England. July 2003. Wheat crop, approximately 250 feet

SILBURY HILL, 2005

The formation at Silbury Hill resembles a huge sea crustacean. Like crabs and lobsters, this creature has ten legs. Note how the body is formed from the almond-shaped vesica. The placement and shapes of the legs are formed by rotational geometry. The circle is first divided into 24 equal sections and then curves are drawn in rotation, which connect various points to one another. These curves not only create the limbs but also the criss-cross pattern that seems to signify the creature's head.

Silbury Hill, Wiltshire, England. July 2005. Wheat crop, approximately 200 feet

Woodborough Hill, Alton Barnes, Wiltshire, England. July 2003. Wheat crop, approximately 180 feet

WOODBOROUGH HILL, ALTON BARNES, 2003

This odd turtle-like formation near Woodborough Hill was a real puzzler. Was it a creature, or something else? The very fine laid square was the first of its kind and although researchers did attempt to rotate the square to see what would happen, we were left none the wiser.

LOCKERIDGE, 1998

This very strange design really did boggle the mind. For some reason, it was nicknamed The Queen. However, whilst this formation is definitely open to any number of interpretations, some even saw a chicken! Locate the triangle pointing towards the top left of the photograph; now consider this piece as the head. This bird is wearing some kind of crown or has a shining countenance. Its eyes are closed as if in a state of contemplation and the standing triangle (pointing downwards) is its beak.

Lockeridge, Wiltshire, England. August 1998. Wheat crop, approximately 200 feet

Clatford Bottom, Wiltshire, England. June 2005. Barley crop, approximately 200 feet

Clatford Bottom, 2005 and Alton Barnes, 2003

These two wonderful formations each depicted three swallows. The Alton Barnes formation (right) showed us three swallows swooping in flight; whilst the Clatford swallows (above) were shown in a circular formation, each with their wing-tips touching. Traditionally, birds signify the spirit. The Alton Barnes birds certainly lifted the spirits of all who came into contact with them and seemed to symbolize the freeing of the spirit. The Clatford birds could signify the three-fold nature of the self: mind, body and spirit. Interestingly, one of these birds was larger than the other two – one can only puzzle over the meaning of such things.

Alton Barnes, Wiltshire, England. August 2003. Wheat crop, approximately 400 feet

CHAPTER SEVEN

MYSTICISM, MYTHOLOGY AND MANDALAS

ARCHETYPAL SYMBOLS

The crop circle designs (more often than not) do not immediately engage the intellect. There are no words, no immediately identifiable language or code and so, in using the tools of our verbal and literal culture, our first interpretations of them are greatly diminished and unequal to the task. Crop circle designs are very seldom obvious or superficial, they are geometric metaphors, similes and allegories. Strictly speaking, therefore, crop circles are symbolic rather than merely signs. Signs are a form of cultural code, an image that substitutes a specific word or phrase. A symbol is much more encompassing; it is a visual embodiment of an archetypal function of truth. Without understanding the symbolic nature of the crop circles, and applying only

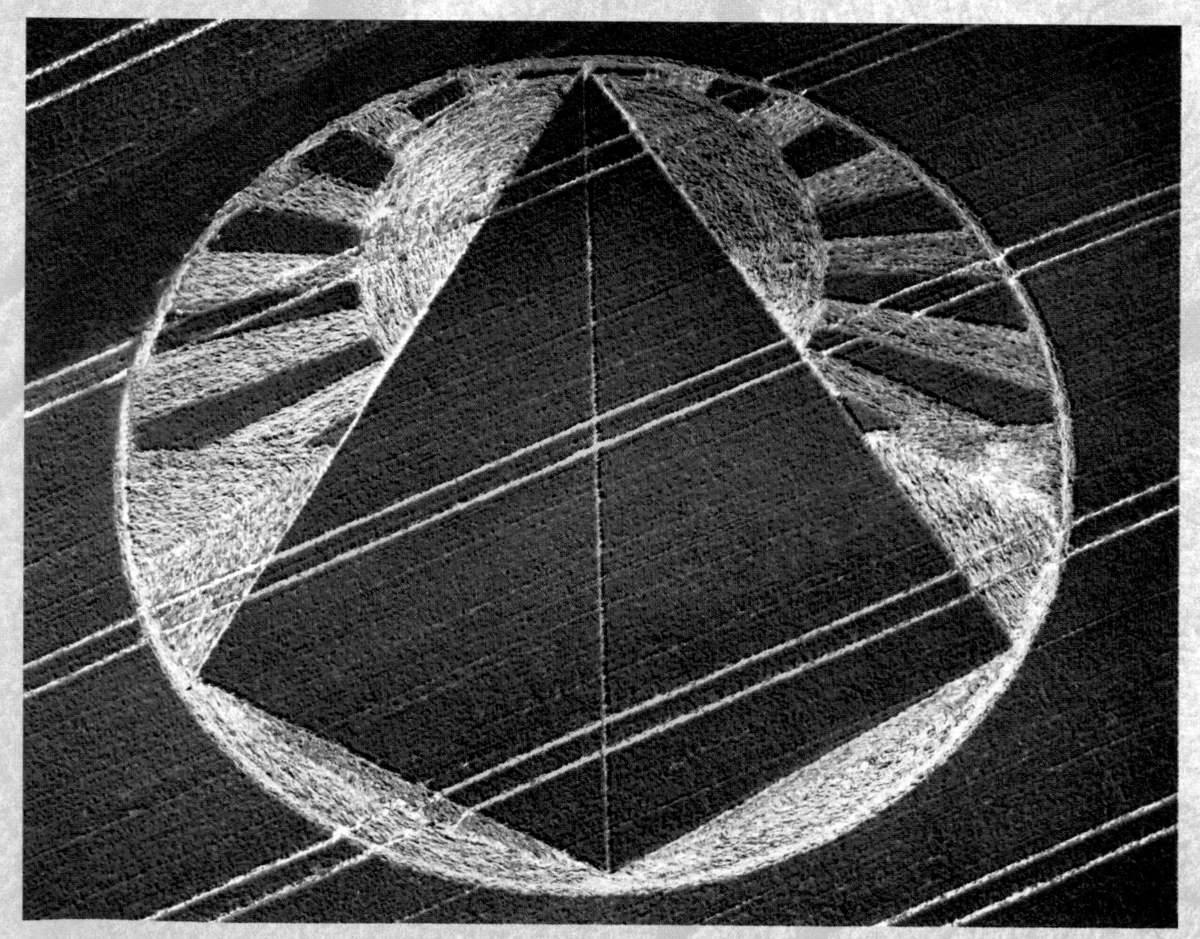

East Field, Alton Barnes, Wiltshire, England. June 2001. Wheat crop, approximately 150 feet

literalism, their designs might be seen as nothing more than arbitrary, pretty or clever. However, when their symbolic nature is embraced, the circles reveal a world rich in meaning and metaphor. It is a straightforward matter of emphasis in perception. A useful approach is to consider the difference between looking at something, in comparison to really seeing it. Suddenly, the world, instead of being full of the mundane, arbitrary, empty and the solely functional, becomes one enriched with significance and patterning. What begins as a way of understanding this mysterious phenomenon becomes a whole new philosophy of perception.

That said, on occasion, the crop circles have presented us with the more familiar; signs and symbols that are already part of our vocabulary. But do not be fooled into reverting to the old literal ways of looking; be prepared to dig a little deeper and see the archetypal principles that are being expressed.

EAST FIELD, ALTON BARNES, 2001 AND HIGHCLERE, 2002

The Alton Barnes pyramid appeared on the morning of the summer solstice 2001; it clearly shows the sun rising over the apex of the pyramid. This was more than a little apt, as the sun also rose exactly over the apex of the Great Pyramid in Giza, Egypt, on the solstice that year. The pyramid at Highclere, just over a year later, was of a different character altogether, this design had clear masonic overtones. For the Freemasons, the pyramid with an eye at its apex represents the all-seeing God, the Grand Architect of the Universe, the brilliance reflects the shining countenance of the divine. The symbol of the all-seeing eye now carries conspiratorial connotations, seen as a metaphor for the New World Order, Big Brother and other such oppressive ideals.

Highclere, Hampshire, England. July 2002. Wheat crop, approximately 200 feet

East Field, Alton Barnes, Wiltshire, England. July 2002. Wheat crop, approximately 180 feet

ALTON BARNES, 2002

The tree at Alton Barnes was compared to many images of the World Tree (*Yggdrasil*) from myth and legend. It is an unusual double image; one way up it is a tree of many fruits with many roots; reversed, it is a mushroom with many spores in the ground. One needs light to grow and ripen its fruit, the other needs darkness to cocoon and nurture the growth of its spores.

BARBURY CASTLE, 1999

There could be no mistaking the menorah design of the crop circle at Barbury Castle. This formation was one of the first to imply the number eleven, with eleven main circles in its design. The curious little pattern that accompanied it perplexed many, but it was suggested that it was a composition of the tools needed to maintain the menorah – oil-lamp, pincers and bowl. The menorah is lit using oil and wicks (not candles), so these items would be used to maintain the flame, a symbol of God's continuing spiritual light.

Barbury Castle, Wiltshire, England. May 1999. Barley crop, approximately 250 feet

BARBURY CASTLE, 1997

Once again, there could be little doubt that this formation depicted the Kabbalistic Ten Sefiroth (Tree of Life). The pattern is a mystical symbol, which shows the forces, principles and functions that underlie the heavenly and earthly realms. The study of this spiritual philosophy is very ancient indeed. Interestingly, the Kabbala is, at root, concerned with the archetypal and the spiritual.

Barbury Castle, Wiltshire, England. May 1997. Oilseed rape (canola) crop, approximately 200 feet

Badbury, Wiltshire, England. June 2001. Barley crop, approximately 200 feet

BADBURY, 2001

This amazing formation showed us the *Ouroboros*. Meaning 'tail-devourer', it shows a serpent eating its own tail. This is a traditional symbol of eternal wisdom, and the cycle of life, death and renewal. However, the design also depicts a turtle or tortoise at its centre. In Hindu mythology, the *Ouroboros* is a dragon who encircles a tortoise, which in turn supports the four elephants that carry the world on their backs.

Inside the snake's body, the crop was woven and knotted. There was also an intricate feathering effect along the inside of the serpent's belly.

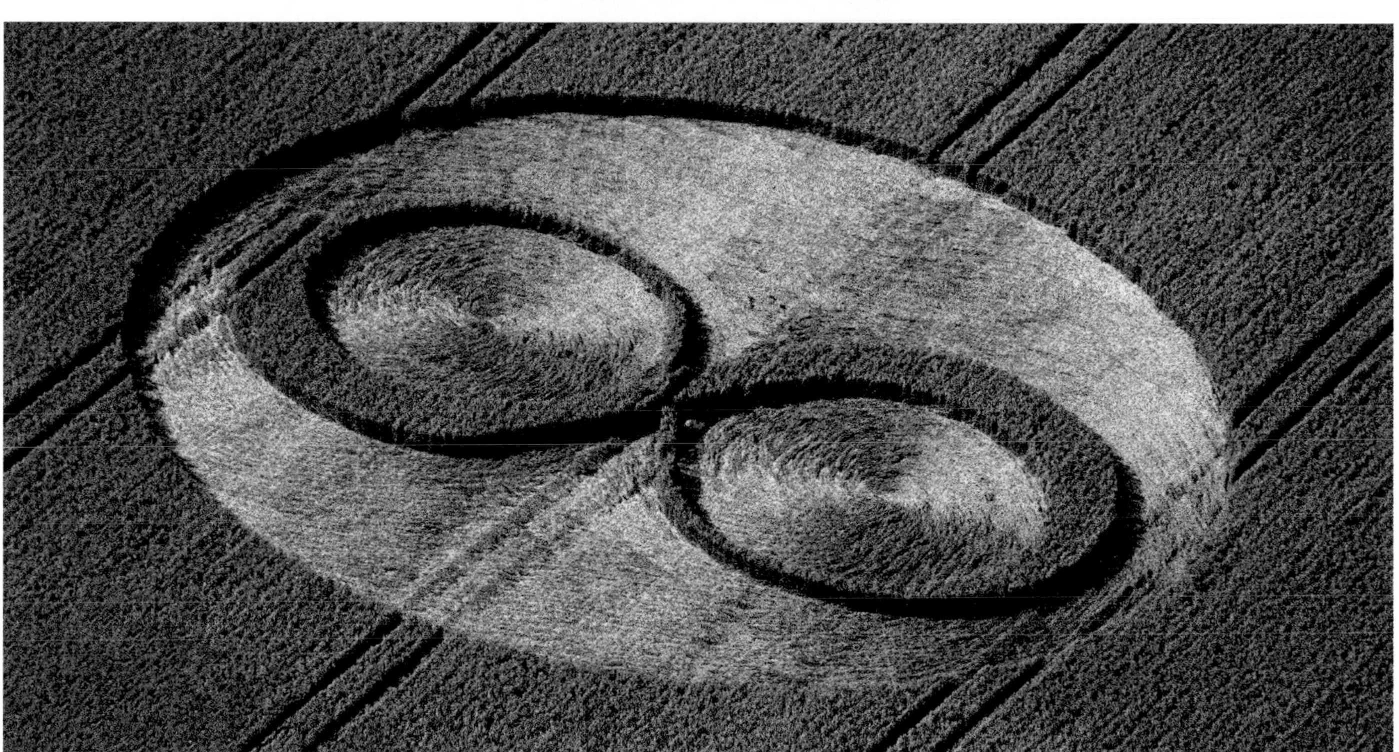

West Overton, Wiltshire, England. July 1994. Wheat crop, approximately 150 feet

WEST OVERTON, 1994

The formation at West Overton might be familiar to us as the lemniscate, or infinity symbol. Looking much like the figure eight on its side, it symbolizes the looping, cyclic and dyadic nature of creation. All photographers will be familiar with this same symbol on the focusing rings of their cameras, indicating the setting for infinity; sometimes the eight-shape appears slightly flattened. The concept of infinity or eternity is one that the crop circles seem to be particularly concerned with, we shall see in our explorations of the fractals, how the circles have taken these concepts to an entirely new level.

MILK HILL, 2004

You might be wondering why this circle did not appear in our section on Forms of Life (page 114). However, whilst this crop formation might at first appear to be some kind of insect, it is undoubtedly an imaginative take on the Caduceus – the winged staff carried by both Hermes (Greek) and Mercury (Roman), messengers of the gods. Traditionally, the staff also has two serpents intertwined along its length – symbols of transformation and renewal.

In modern times, the winged staff has become an international symbol of the healing arts and medicine. Many pharmaceutical companies, hospitals and surgeries display the Caduceus.

The tentative suggestion of the messenger of the gods being at work in our crop fields is a seductive one, but more than that, it goes to show, yet again, how intimately these symbols are connected to our myths, legends and ultimately, to our psyche.

Milk Hill, Wiltshire, England. June 2004. Wheat crop, approximately 600 feet

Barbury Castle, Wiltshire, England. July 2003. Wheat crop, approximately 400 feet

Alton Priors, Wiltshire, England. August 2001. Wheat crop, approximately 180 feet

MANDALAS

HEALING THE LANDSCAPE AND THE MIND

Mandalas (Sanskrit for 'circle') are another form of archetypal symbolism. We traditionally think of them as spiritual devices, used in the contemplation of the patterns and forces which underlie creation. The seeker meditatively enters the patterns – conventionally a square enclosed within a circle – tracing the lines and forms in search of insight or stillness from the chatter of the mind. The design of these ritual mandalas is essentially based on some of the geometric philosophy we have explored in this book; many combine the circle and the square, symbolic of the meeting of man and the Divine. There is however, another form of mandala, perhaps less well-known, and it might be called 'mandala of the mind'. It was the psychoanalyst Carl Jung who first recognized the importance and significance of mandalas. His patients would often draw or dream of circular patterns, inside which many chaotic elements would be contained. Jung saw these patterns as images of the self, and noted that as these patients began to progress in their therapy, so these once chaotic images would become progressively more ordered. Many crop circles could be classified as mandalas; perhaps they heal both us and our sometimes beleaguered and chaotic world.

ALTON PRIORS, 2001 AND BARBURY CASTLE, 2003

These classic mandala-like designs are based on four-fold and six-fold geometry respectively. Each divides the whole (or circle) equally and precisely. The simple order of design is pleasing to the eye, almost comforting and reassuring. Have you ever noticed how much asymmetry can irk the mind: that picture that isn't straight on the wall; that something that seems out of place? Some of us can live with a little more disorder than others, but too much disarray can be uncomfortable, even troubling.

(ABOVE) *Liddington Castle, Wiltshire, England. July 1999. Wheat crop, approximately 150 feet*
(BELOW) *Chisbury, Wiltshire, England. July 2003. Wheat crop, approxomately 200 feet*

LIDDINGTON CASTLE, 1999 AND CHISBURY, 2003

These two pleasing designs fall into the category of mandalas. The formation at Liddington Castle (right) is a three-fold design, the level and order and symmetry is detailed and a touch mechanical. It looks like a cog from some unknown machine. The Chisbury formation (below) is almost its dyadic opposite. Here six-fold geometry is at work, but the pattern is based entirely on circular geometry, giving the details of this design a lace-like feel. Notice how the floor-lay of the outer ring of the Chisbury circle is woven into a fish-bone design.

AVEBURY HENGE, 2002

This lovely mandala explores contrast – light and dark, standing and flattened, Yin (dark) and Yang (light). In the traditional rendering of the Yin-Yang symbol, each contains a little of the other and the two symbols spiral around, chasing each other to find a resolution, to become one.

Yin-Yang also represents the masculine and feminine in all of us. It tells us that we each have both of these principles within us and that both fit together perfectly to create one whole – the Yin-Yang symbols combine to create a circular mandala.

Avebury Henge, Wiltshire, England. July 2002. Wheat crop, approximately 300 feet

CHAPTER EIGHT

STARS, MOONS AND PLANETS

HEAVENLY BODIES

For thousands of years man has looked up to the heavens and gazed upon the stars. He has been guided by the position of stars when navigating the earth and, for some, man's fate is encoded in the constellations and their planetary aspects. The planets were dedicated to ancient gods, or became their heavenly embodiment in the night sky – Mars the God of War and Venus the Goddess of Love.

The sun and the moon have always been accorded special veneration. One governs our day, the other our night; one governs our (lunar) months, the other our (solar) years. The sun is generally associated with masculinity, brilliant and strong but sometimes severe and harsh; whereas the moon is associated with the feminine, coy and beautiful but at times driving one to lunacy! In alchemy, the metal ascribed to the sun was gold, and silver for the moon; the eclipse of the two signified the marriage of Heaven and Earth.

As many television science programmes seem fond of telling us, we ourselves are made of the stuff of stars. Scientists also theorize that life itself many have been borne here on asteroids or comets that collided with Earth. The symbolism seems particularly apt: the comet with its shimmering, gaseous tail, piercing the beautiful spherical Earth, giving rise to life on our planet, just as the sperm breaches the egg in order to initiate a human life.

Ancient Egyptian texts tell us the Pharaohs believed that after death their souls would be propelled into the night sky to dwell with their gods, who inhabited the twinkling firmament. According to one popular theory, they may have even built their pyramids to mirror the stars. Many ancient peoples were in awe of the sky and her heavenly bodies; their gods told them when to sow their crops and when to harvest them; predicting times of plenty and the onset of the cold, harsh, winter months.

Human culture has been intimately linked to the stars, moon and planets since civilization began. That we see them described by the crop circles is fascinating, but they are yet another archetypal theme as relevant to our psychological make-up as those of number, shape, labyrinths, mazes, threads and tethers. Over the years, the crop circles have given us stars, moons, planets, eclipses, asteroid belts and galaxies to contemplate.

Silbury Hill, Wiltshire, England. August 2002. Wheat crop, approximately 200 feet

West Kennett longbarrow, Wiltshire, England. July 2004. Wheat crop, approximately 180 feet

WEST KENNETT LONGBARROW, 2004 AND SILBURY HILL, 2002

The star at Silbury Hill was a classic pentagram, whilst the sun and moon at West Kennett seemed like a design depicting an eclipse. However, look carefully at the interior floor-lay of the West Kennett formation and you will see that a tiny swirl of crop appears inside it; the timing of the crop circle coincided with the transit of Venus across the sun during June 2004. Therefore, this circle could be showing the profile of Venus as it traversed the face of the sun that summer. The next time this kind of celestial phenomenon occurs will be 6 June 2012.

PEWSEY, 2000

This lovely formation showed a central circle containing three standing stars, with a narrow crescent moon (or Cheshire-cat smile). A very narrow outer ring then holds an orbiting circle. Notice a tiny, barely visible ring of standing crop in the orbiting circle. It was described by visitors as being beautifully delicate and crown-like.

Pewsey, Wiltshire, England. August 2000. Wheat crop, approximately 150 feet

SILBURY HILL, 2000

This group of six pentagrams was notable for the fact that one star seemed to be deformed. This circle was quickly nicknamed the Stargate Formation, as it appeared that one of the points had been moved aside to grant access to the interior of the star.

Silbury Hill, Wiltshire, England. July 2000. Wheat crop, approximately 250 feet

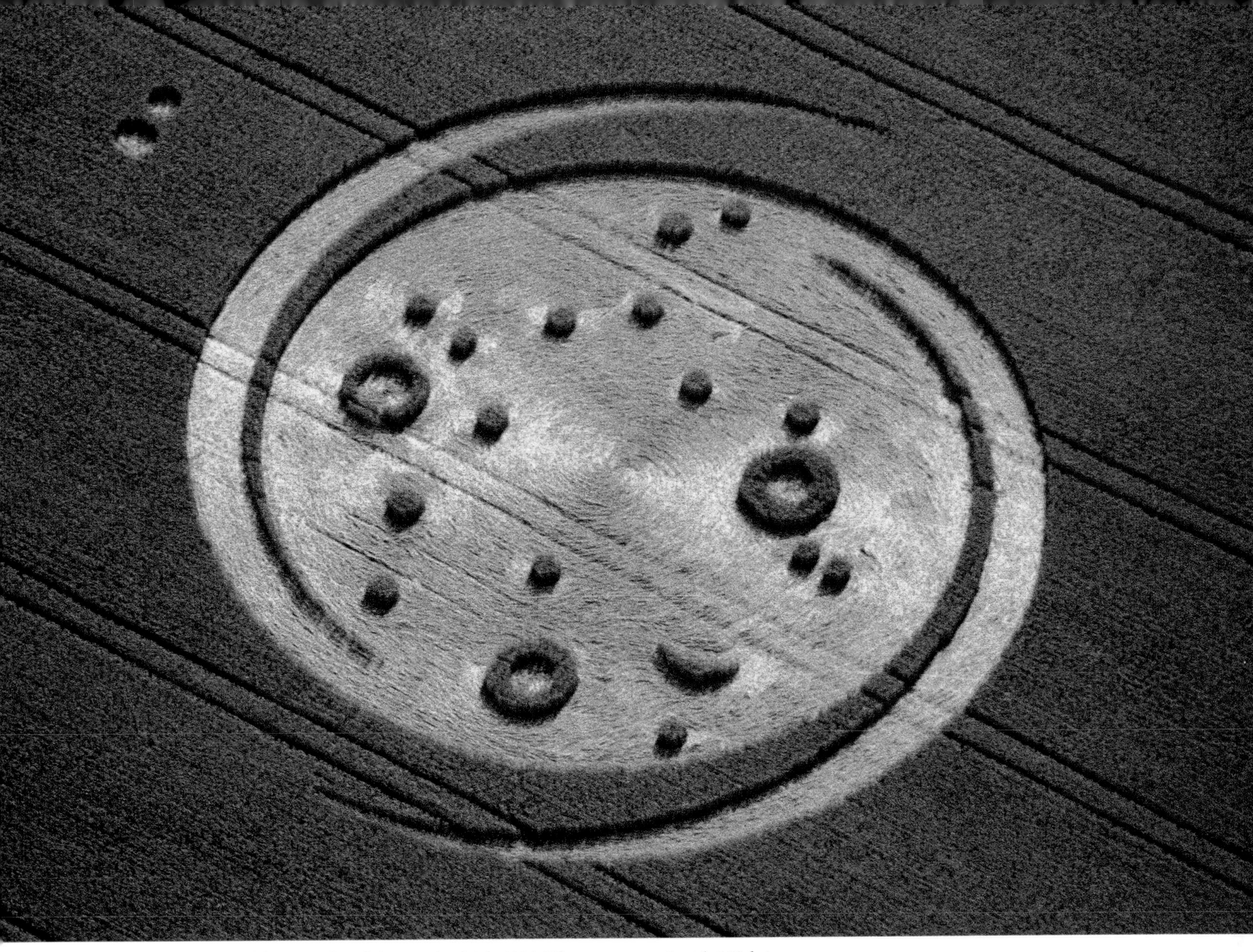

(ABOVE AND BELOW) *West Stowell, Wiltshire, England. July 1994. Wheat crop, approximately 180 feet*

WEST STOWELL, 1994

The Galaxy at West Stowell was not the first of its kind. There had been another earlier on in the year, near Avebury. However, the farmer decided to cut out the interior of that formation before any aerial pictures could be taken and its interior design is now only discernable from ground shots taken by prompt researchers. This second galaxy design was wonderful on the ground, the fallen wheat created a water-like flow around the various standing elements, like a fine translucent fabric holding the formation together.

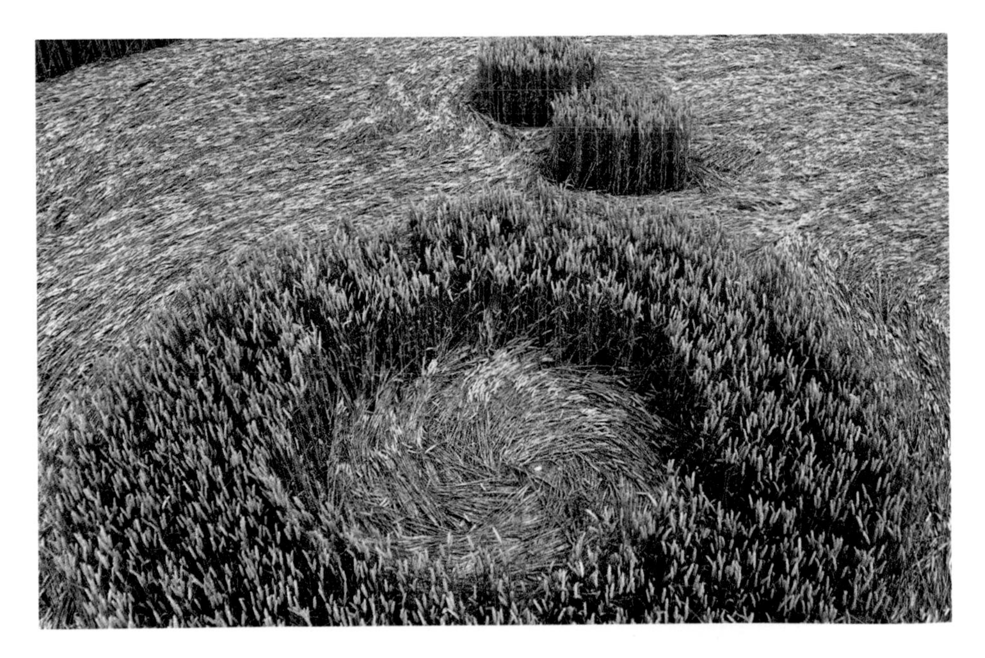

BISHOPS SUTTON, 1995

1995 was the year of the asteroid belt formations. This formation contained 99 individual circles with one ringed circle and two narrow orbit-like rings around which the whole design was arranged. Each circle was beautifully made, with a variety of swirls and standing central tufts incorporated to make the experience on the ground every bit as awe inspiring as the view from the air. The formation was placed on a sloping field and could be seen from the local main road.

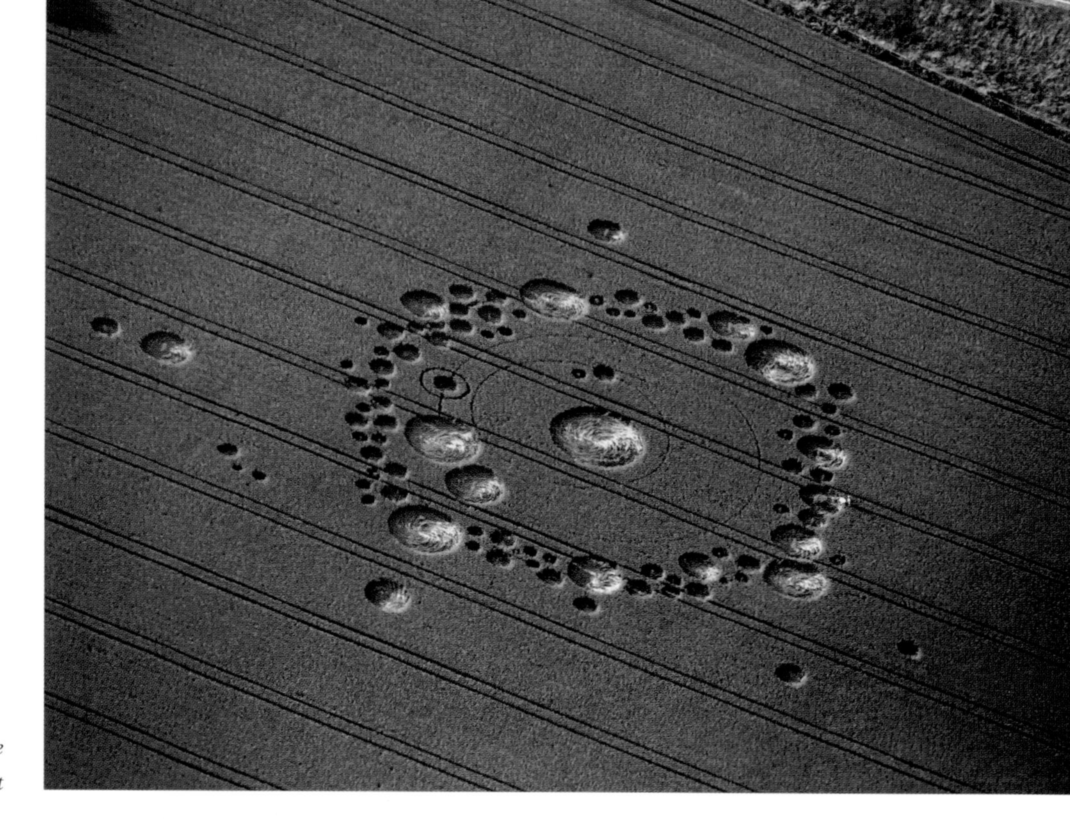

(RIGHT) *Bishops Sutton, Hampshire, England. June 1995. Wheat crop, approximately 250 feet*

LONGWOOD WARREN, 1995

The formation at Longwood Warren was the culmination of the 1995 season and was undoubtedly a representation of our inner solar system. However, it was quickly observed that planet Earth had been left out and so it was called the Earth-is-missing Formation. To some this was a matter of grave concern, interpreting the crop circle as a messenger of doom; to others it signified nothing more than the fact that the circle was located on planet Earth. This design clearly shows the sun at the centre, with Mercury, then Venus; there is an orbit indicated for the Earth; then Mars is shown; the whole thing is ringed by a string of circles, representing the asteroid belt that separates the inner planets from the outer ones.

Longwood Warren, Hampshire, England. June 1995. Wheat crop, approximately 350 feet

East Meon, 1995

The beautiful East Meon crescents were another product of the 1995 season. This type of nested crescent motif has been used many times by the circle-makers, always to great effect. However, this is perhaps its most accomplished incarnation. Two central rings are surrounded by six crescents, three standing and three flattened; the whole design is then contained in one large ring. Apart from the striking design (based entirely on circular geometry) what made this formation particularly interesting was its placement in the landscape.

From the photograph you can clearly see how the centre of this circle is placed on a tractor line which meets a natural break in the tree line at the side of the field. This kind of harmony and consideration for placement in the landscape significantly enhances the experience of walking the interior space. The synchronicity of such meaningful positioning can have a very marked effect on the mind, leading one to contemplate the reasoning behind such attention to detail.

(ABOVE AND BELOW) *East Meon, Hampshire, England. July 1995. Wheat crop, approximately 200 feet*

Middle Wallop, Hampshire, England. May 1999.
Oilseed rape (canola) crop, approximately 400 feet

SUN, MOON, ECLIPSE AND A STAR

During the summer of 1994, two formations appeared on the same night in different, but adjoining, fields at East Dean in Sussex (below and below far right). One contained a ringed sun-like disc, the other a crescent moon. They appeared to be chasing one another across the fields, just like the sun and moon eternally chase one another to create night and day. In 1999 (the year of the latest full solar eclipse in the UK) an amazing formation appeared at Middle Wallop in Hampshire, which seemed to depict the various stages of an eclipse (left). The golden yellow of the oilseed rape (canola) crop seemed to highlight the solar aspect of this heavenly event. Finally, at Beckhampton, a constellation of moons appeared locked in place by a pentagram and a ring with five equal divisions (far right). What celestial occasion might this design allude to? We may never know.

East Dean, Sussex, England. July 1994. Barley crop, approximately 300 feet

(ABOVE) *Beckhampton, Wiltshire, England. July 2003. Wheat crop, approximately 250 feet*

East Dean, Sussex, England. July 1994. Wheat crop, approximately 300 feet

CHAPTER NINE

THE FRACTALS

INFINITE ITERATIONS

Beautiful filigrees of immeasurable depth and complexity, fractals are strangely mesmerising. They can appear as undulating landscapes of the finest lace, woven veils of shape and pattern, self-similar variations upon a theme; seemingly multidimensional and holographic. This relatively modern branch of mathematics fuses number, space and colour to make visible the peculiar world of abstract number functions.

The term 'fractal' was first coined in the mid-1970s by Benoît Mandlebrot, the father of modern fractals, and was derived from the Latin word *fractus*, which means broken or irregular. The concept of fractals had long been known about before Mandlebrot, but it was his innovatory use of computers to generate, plot and visually display the outcome of the millions of recursive calculations necessary for complex fractals that gave birth to the contemporary era of fractal mathematics and fractal geometry.

The importance of his discovery is hard to overstate. Fractal geometry gave mathematicians and scientists a feasible model for calculating such things as the length of an infinitesimally complex coastline, and the various branching systems found throughout the natural world. Fractals were able to simulate accurately, for the first time, the complex shapes of clouds and even the blood circulatory system of the human body. Modern fractal mathematics was able to generate and then map the tiny variations created by the recursive iteration of simple number equations, so as to create a viable imitation of the slightly imperfect and sometimes random fluctuations of the natural world; something which that had thus so far eluded both science and mathematics.

The computer generation of fractals has seen entire mountain ranges and even the unfurling fronds of fern leaves appear simulated on computer screens, demonstrating their fascinating potential to teach us about nature and the processes of generation and creation.

Fractals have several important core properties. First is their use of self-similarity. At their most basic, they can be a repetition of a single shape, but on differing scales. In the Koch Snowflake, for example, an infinite number of triangular shapes that progressively diminish in size are continually added to the perimeter of its shape. This means that the snowflake has an infinite boundary, whilst in principle its area remains finite. This last property is another important aspect of fractal geometry. They occupy a bizarre space that holds together the opposing concepts of the infinite and the finite in one location. Not only is this a mathematical paradox, it also has fascinating mystical connotations. The fractal beautifully and succinctly illustrates a vision of a single finite creation, at the heart of which lies infinite free-will and choice. Finally, another important property of fractals is their ability to present a tangible visualization of infinity. No matter how much a fractal image is magnified, one always finds self-similar repetitions of the original fractal shape at every level. To dive headlong into these realms is to come face-to-face with eternity made manifest.

However, far from being abstract, fractal geometry plays an important role in the modern world. It sits at the hub of computer-generated imagery (CGI) which creates special effects for the film industry, and is also used in the compression of digital photographic images.

The Mandlebrot Set, Ickleton, Cambridgeshire. August 1991. Wheat crop, approximately 230 feet

THE ICKLETON MANDLEBROT SET, 1991

'A heart with complications' was how this crop circle was first described when reported: it was a beautiful golden cardioid form in a field of wheat, close to Ickleton in Cambridgeshire. It was quickly identified as a Mandlebrot Set fractal.

The Mandlebrot is the fractal of fractals: whilst there are many versions of other fractal types, there is only one Mandlebrot Set. The use of such a complex and relatively unheard of branch of mathematics in a crop circle design was uncanny, to say the least – as was the fact that the circle lay not far from where Mandlebrot had discovered his fractal, in Cambridge.

STONEHENGE JULIA SET, 1996

Along with the Ickleton Mandlebrot, the Stonehenge Julia Set Fractal is regarded as one of the greatest classic crop circle formations. It is very closely related to the Mandelbrot Set, in that it is generated when a small variation is added to the calculations used to generate the Mandelbrot Set. The Julia Set manifests as a shape containing iterations of interconnecting spiral-like elements.

Whereas the Ickleton Mandlebrot had been fairly modest in scale, the Stonehenge Julia Set was simply huge in comparison. It measured 915 feet along the length of the curve and contained 151 circles, all varying in diameter.

Some geometers have claimed that the Julia curve was a Golden Section spiral, but this was not borne out by surveys carried out on the design in the field; the nature of the spiral is as yet unclassified. There are also several subtle design components that make this crop circle a truly amazing work of art. The circles that comprise the main spiral-curve of the formation vary in size. Interestingly they are largest where the curve is at its most acute. Not only does this accentuate the line of the curve, but it was also discovered that the largest circles sat on the highest point of the ground, and, as the ground sloped downward, so the circles correspondingly reduced in size. This significant detail shows the intricate way in which some crop circles are linked to the topography and landscape – a fact not frequently acknowledged.

However, the most startling aspect of the formation was its placement adjacent to the ancient stone circle, Stonehenge. The juxtaposition of the ancient geometry used in the construction of Stonehenge and the ultra-modern fractal geometry expressed by the crop circle was a potent symbolic gesture that magically bound together the ancient and the modern worlds.

(ABOVE AND RIGHT) *The Stonehenge Julia Set fractal, Wiltshire, England. July 1996. Wheat crop, approximately 915 feet along the spine*

WINDMILL HILL, 1996
AND EAST FIELD, ALTON BARNES, 1996

Despite its complex nature, the Stonehenge Julia was the second in a family of three major formations to appear that year. Beginning on 17 June, a huge string of 89 circles that resembled the human DNA helix had appeared in Alton Barnes; 7 July had seen the arrival of the Stonehenge Julia fractal; and on 29 July, a huge triple-armed spiral containing 194 circles appeared at a place called Windmill Hill and was soon named the Triple Julia, because of the seeming similarity between the Stonehenge and Windmill Hill formations. However, in fractal geometry there is no such thing as a 'triple Julia set', and closer inspection of the formations reveals that the curves involved in the Windmill Hill formation are nowhere near as acute as that of the Stonehenge fractal.

Although only one of the three formations appeared to be a true fractal, they nevertheless had several features in common that called for them to be grouped together. First was their exclusive use of circles to achieve their overall design, and, more specifically, the use of many relatively small circles compared to the size of the overall pattern. Second, there was the number of circles in the designs. Never before had so many individual elements been used to create a crop circle pattern – this lead to the idea of a 'crop formation'.

The Triple Julia Set, Windmill Hill, Wiltshire, England. July 1996. Wheat crop, approximately 700 feet

(ABOVE) East Field, Alton Barnes, Wiltshire, England. June 1996. Barley crop, approximately 650 feet

(LEFT) Inside the Triple Julia Set (see far left)

Lastly, there was the overall magnitude of these formations – from 648 feet for the DNA Helix, to the 915 feet for the Stonehenge Julia, and just slightly under 700 feet for Windmill Hill.

Some have postulated that DNA uses self-similarity (a fractal-like property) to enable it to store huge amounts of information in one tiny vessel. So these formations may ultimately have more to their relationship than similarity in construction.

The so-called Triple Julia was so large that one visitor was actually able to ride his bicycle through the formation. Like so many of the formations, the design was utterly incomprehensible from the ground – only the aerial photographs could finally reveal the amazing totality of the structure.

SiLBURY HiLL, 1997 AND MiLK HiLL, 1997

During 1997, an amazing miracle occurred – we had beautiful snowflakes falling at the height of the summer heat! These amazing formations were unmistakeably Koch Snowflakes, a type of fractal first described in the early 1900s by Helge Von Koch, a Swedish mathematician. The Koch Snowflake is one of the simplest varieties of fractals. Most fractals, such as the Mandlebrot and Julia Sets are impossible to draw on paper; the calculations involved in their construction are simply vast and the points needed to plot the shapes are often so small as to be beyond the visible. However, although we might only be able to plot several iterations of the Koch Snowflake before they become too small for the pencil to draw accurately, it is possible for us to begin to understand the basic principles of fractal geometry.

The Koch Snowflake essentially deals with divisions of a triangle. Beginning with one equilateral triangle, the length of each side is divided by three and a smaller triangle (one third the size of the original) is added to the centre of each of the three sides of our starting triangle. The result of this first iteration is the creation of a Star of David shape. The process is then repeated with even smaller triangles (each a third the size of the previous iteration) added to the middle of each side, until the triangles become so small that no further iterations can be drawn by hand. This very simple exercise generates a shape whose perimeter may carry on ad infinitum, becoming progressively more complex (and therefore longer), but whose core internal area remains largely unchanged – in other words, we create a shape with a genuine paradox of properties.

Koch Snowflake, Silbury Hill, Wiltshire, England. July 1997. Wheat crop, approximately 300 feet

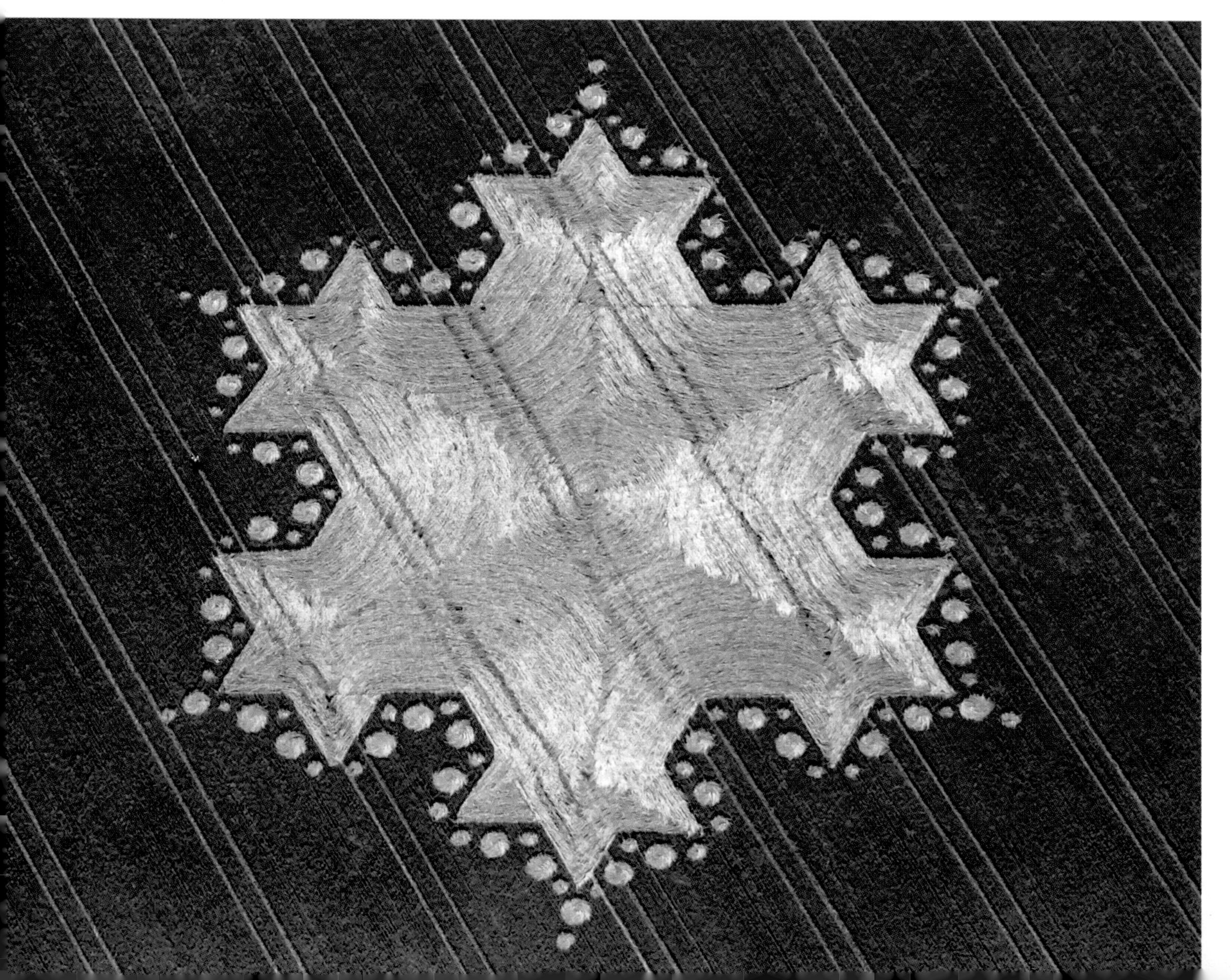

The first Snowflake to occur was close to Silbury Hill. At the time, this formation held the record for containing the largest area of flattened crop ever recorded in a crop circle – it was calculated to be no less than 0.86 acres. Although the crop circle showed only three iterations of the Koch fractal, the small circles around its perimeter were thought to be symbolic of further implied iterations. The floor-lay of the crop led to more surprise; from the air, the interior of the circle created the impression of a three-dimensional object – a spider's web pattern visible in the flattened crop – the first time this had been seen in a formation.

The second Snowflake (below) was the pinnacle of that year, appearing at Milk Hill, near Alton Barnes. This time the design contained a beautiful feature at its centre, a kind of inside-out Koch Snowflake. Once again, small circles surrounded the main design. Each was unique and beautifully crafted; some had standing centres, and others had knots and nests of swirled wheat stems. The laid crop of this second Snowflake had qualities reminiscent of flowing water.

Inside the Milk Hill Snowflake

Koch II Snowflake, Milk Hill, Wiltshire, England. July 1997. Wheat crop, approximately 350 feet

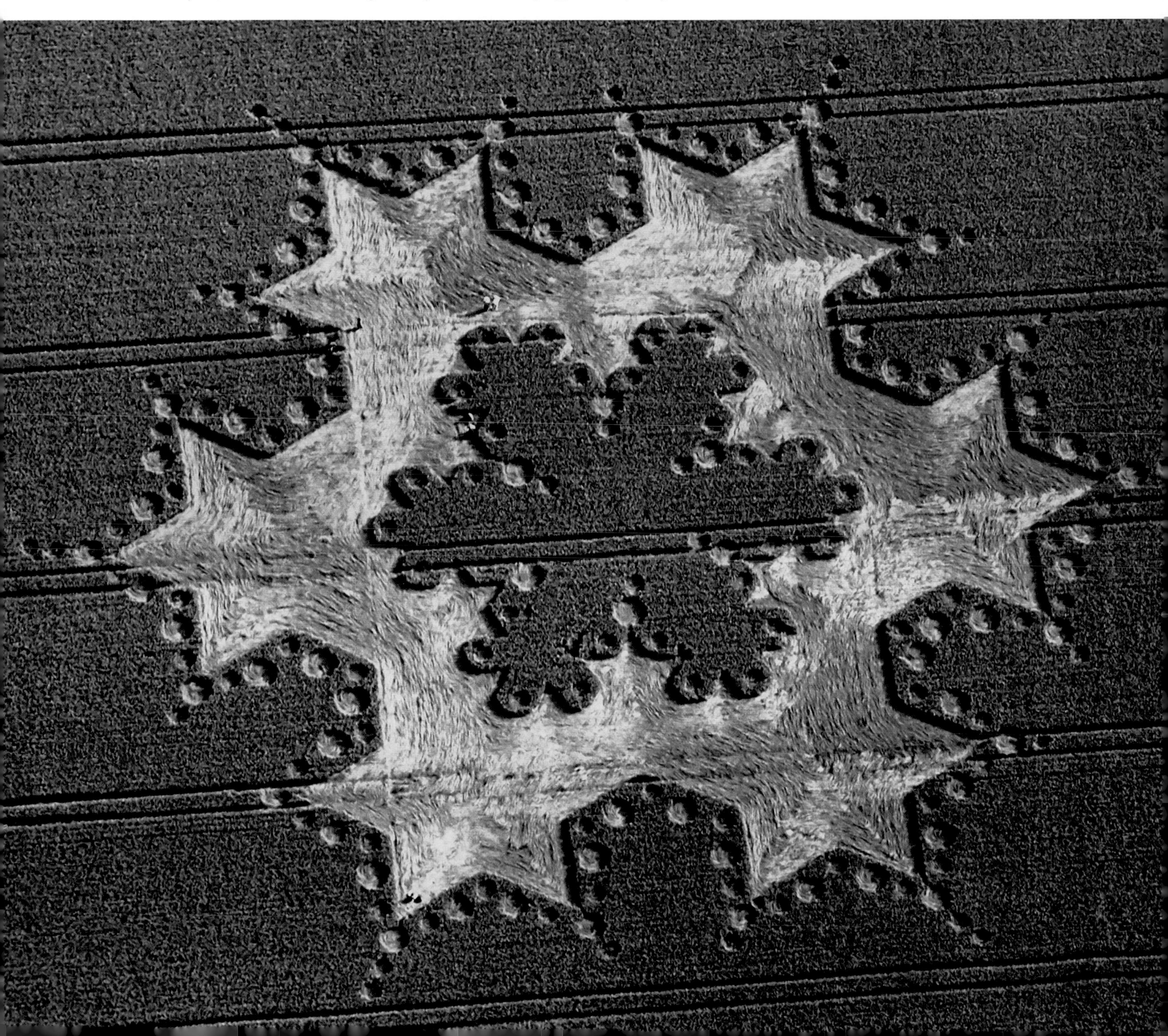

Silbury Hill, Wiltshire, England. July 1999. Wheat crop, approximately 275 feet

SILBURY HILL, 1999

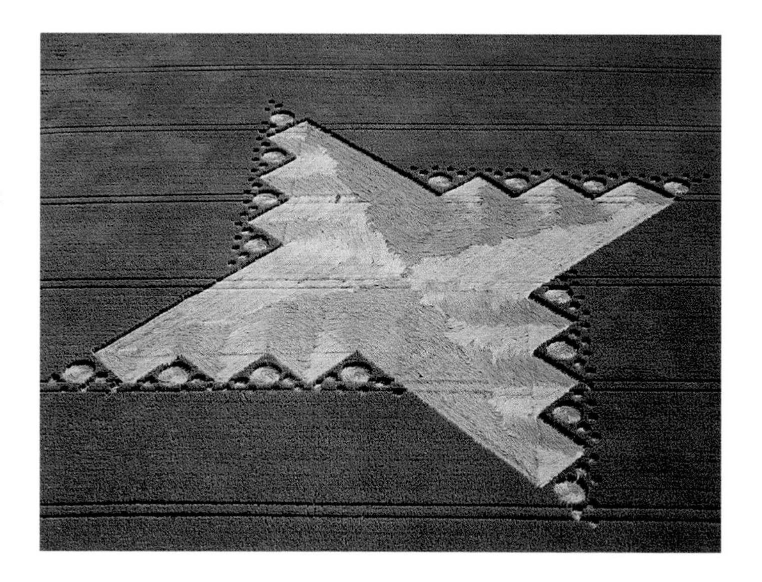

Along with the many true fractals that have appeared as crop circles, there are a number of other crop circles that, whilst not true fractals, are nevertheless of the same family type – or are 'fractal-esque'. This amazing formation appeared close to Silbury Hill on 24th July 1999 and measured around 275 feet across its diagonal.

Here, the zigzag edges on each opposing arm are reminiscent of the outer edges of the Koch Snowflakes of 1997, and they even have the accompanying tiny circles, which seem to represent further iterations of shape. Once again, the vast interior expanse of this formation was flattened in such a way as to create a secondary pattern in the laid crop, appreciable only from the air. So, while not a fractal in the strict mathematical sense, these formations use fractal-like characteristics in their design.

(LEFT) *West Kennett, Wiltshire, England. August 1999. Wheat crop, approximately 250 feet*

(BELOW) *Windmill Hill, Wiltshire, England. July 1999. Wheat crop, approximately 320 feet*

WINDMILL HILL, 1999 AND WEST KENNETT, 1999

Reminiscent of a the floor design of a great fortress or temple, these two formations are based on the principle of ever-decreasing squares. Like the Koch Snowflakes, the re-iteration of smaller and smaller squares is then finished off with small circles to imply a continuation of this process. Both of these formations deal with the same core shapes; one is, in a loose sense, an inversion of the other.

Both formations appeared close to the megalithic stone burial chamber at West Kennett.

Notice, once again, the interior floor of the West Kennett formation and its three-dimensional effect. This could almost be a set of nested pyramids, rather than squares.

CHILBOLTON, 1999 AND FARLEY MOUNT, 2002

This diamond-shaped formation (below) is a representation of a Sierspinski Gasket, another fractal that uses nested triangles to create a triangular or diamond shape. Incidentally, the Sierspinski Gasket is now the pattern for the internal aerials of mobile telephones, because it offers one of the best ways to achieve the largest aerial area in a confined space – a good example of the practical use of fractal geometry.

The branches of the pretty little tree at Farley Mount (right) are divided using ever-decreasing iterations of the Golden Section.

Farley Mount, Hampshire, England. August 2002. Wheat crop, approximately 120 feet

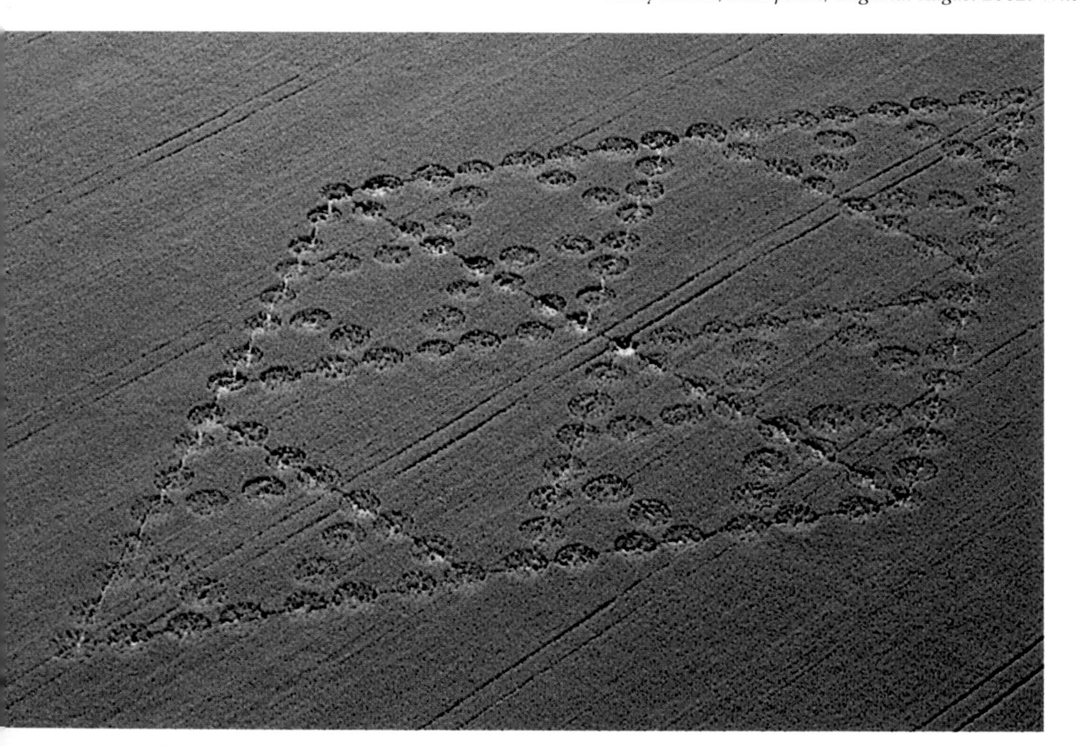

Chilbolton, Hampshire, England. June 1999. Barley crop, approximately 340 feet

CLIFFORD'S HILL, 2001

In this pattern (right), two equal circles are fitted exactly into a larger one. Combined, the two smaller circles have exactly the same perimeter length as the outer circle. This continuous division into two has a cumulative result, with the sum of the perimeters of all the smaller contained circles in each section being equal to that of the original containing circle. Theoretically, divisions can go on indefinitely until the curves of circles across the diameter become so minute that they are virtually indiscernable – and that is how a curved line appears straight.

(RIGHT) Clifford's Hill, Wiltshire, England. July 2001. Wheat crop, approximately 200 feet

WINDMILL HILL, 2001

This harmonious formation appeared on 14 July 2001 beneath Windmill Hill, and was part of a closely-related pair. There is something beautifully harmonious about this formation – it displayed an exquisite play on circles and curves, which was a running theme of the 2001 season. During any given season, themes can occur, which are then worked through and brought to a final resolution over several different formations. These circles are often labelled as siblings or family groups. Undulating through the centre of this particular formation is water-like wave, which is key to its fractal-like properties. This circle uses a series of three self-similar shapes, diminishing in size, to create the overall design.

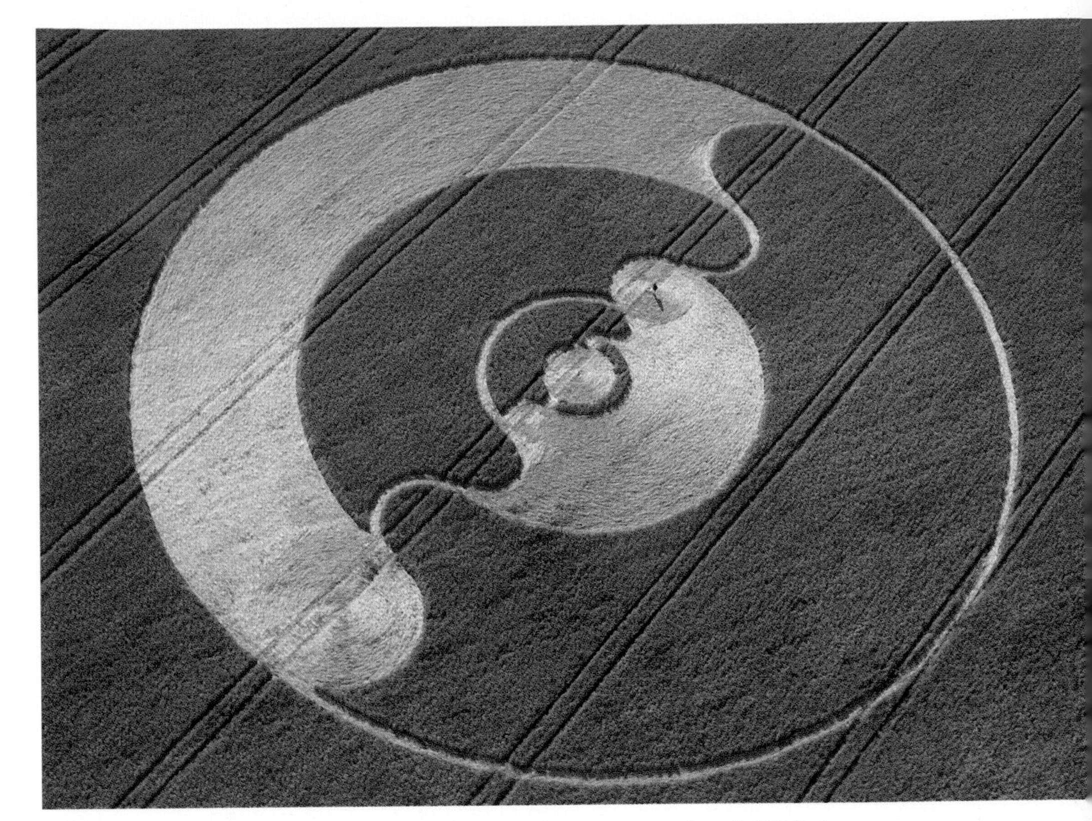

(ABOVE) *Windmill Hill, Wiltshire, England. July 2001. Wheat crop, approximately 200 feet*

ALTON BARNES, 2005

This spectacular formation appeared in the natural amphitheatre of East Field in Alton Barnes, Wiltshire. Once again, this design is not a true fractal, but it does have fractal-esque features.

Two successive pairs of diminishing squares create the main bulk of the formation. However, as we travel towards the middle of the formation, something unexpected happens. Another fractal-like square shape is implied at the very centre, surrounded by an incredible collection of complex squares and oblongs.

From a subjective point of view, this formation seemed to speak of fragmentation and simultaneous evolution of form.

Notice the tiny boxes around the perimeter, reminiscent of the Koch Snowflake designs of 1997 (see pages 150 and 151).

East Field, Alton Barnes, Wiltshire, England. July 2005. Wheat crop, approximately 350 feet

THE INTERFACE PATTERNS

The crop circles have at times presented us with formations that suggest some kind of energy field or system, interference patterns or waves. The meaning of these patterns is unknown but they are often intricate and fascinating. While most circles combine geometric forms in a conventional manner, these shapes make use of the partial or total integration of two or more shapes to create wave-like configurations. Perhaps they are suggestive of the waves of subtle energy created by the shape itself.

Shalbourne, Wiltshire, England. August 2004. Approximately 200 feet

SHALBOURNE, 2004

Created by the partial intersection of two circles (or sets of concentric rings), this looks like the wave patterns generated in a still pool by two droplets of water falling onto its surface.

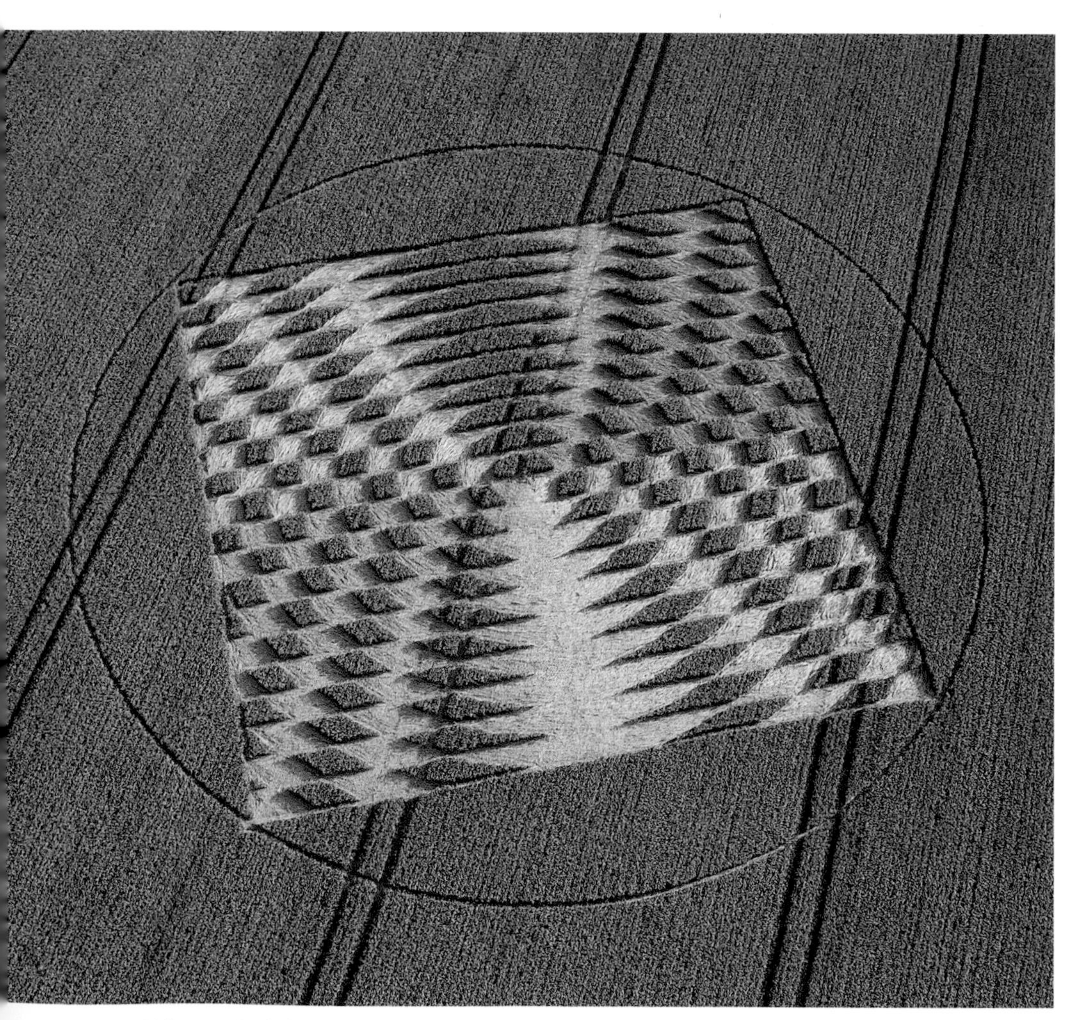

Aldbourne, Wiltshire, England. July 2005. Wheat crop. Approximately 200 feet.

ALDBOURNE, 2005

This seems to open a window upon what could be a larger pattern, the rest of which is concealed from view. Geometrically, it is a combination of many narrow concentric rings and a set of narrow lines running horizontally across them. It is, in fact, a synergy of the circle and the line. Symbolically, this formation is particularly interesting; the circle is connected to one-ness and the line to two-ness. The development from one to two brings about opposition, and we can see from the pattern that each half is a mirror opposite of the other. This circle seems to show this process at work.

Shalbourne, Wiltshire, England. August 2005. Wheat crop. 250 feet

SHALBOURNE, 2005

This pattern is based on the superimposition of two sets of very narrow concentric rings; the final effect looks like light shining off the surface of a flat disc. Perhaps all these formations are concerned with the relationship between energy systems, shape and number.

CHAPTER TEN

INTERNATIONAL CIRCLES

CULTURAL DIVERSITY

The crop circles are not a phenomenon confined to England or indeed even the UK; they are reported each year from all over the globe. However, it is true to say that the Wiltshire area of the UK is the world centre for crop circles. With its numerous ancient sites, it seems that the circles feel most at home here. Many reasons for this have been put forward over the years, among them, the chalk downland, the underground aquifers, and a concentration of earth energies. But perhaps what this part of the world offers is a synchronous combination of many factors.

The designs of the crop circles seem to be culturally specific. Those of the US appear to be attracted to Native American sites and their designs are markedly different in style and 'feel' from those of the UK. European formations, while similar to those in the UK, also have a style and atmosphere of their own and are likewise often connected to megalithic sites.

The number of circles that appear in other countries is difficult to calculate with accuracy. In a huge country such as the US, many circles may appear each year never to be reported. Sometimes they are not discovered until the harvester is upon them, and some farmers consider the crop circles an interminable nuisance, so deliberately neglect to mention them. In somewhere as large as the US it would be quite an operation to set up a network of well-placed researchers to cover the whole country. In a small country such as the UK it becomes more manageable. The best way to record the circles is to photograph them from the air, but once again the logistical problems, as well as the considerable financial cost involved, multiply considerably when operating on a larger scale.

We have assembled a montage of circles from outside the UK, to give you a taste of what is happening elsewhere.

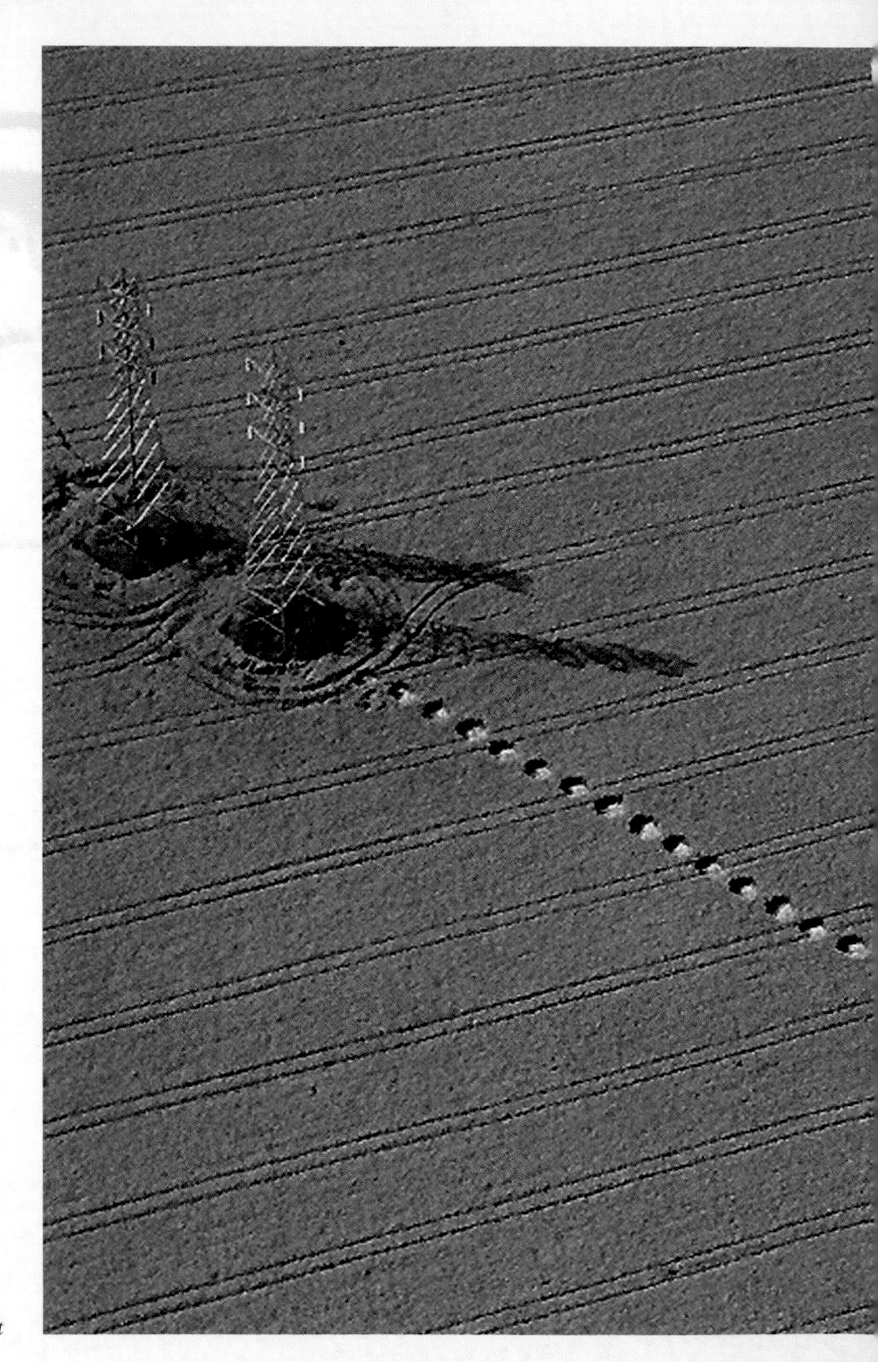

Fairfield, California, USA. June 2004. Wheat crop, approximately 300 ft

USA AND CANADA

It is clear from these six images how different crop circle designs are in the US and Canada, compared to the UK. The huge formation in Fairfield, CA, (previous page) was a beautiful design, perhaps another form of life. Its long tail was a line of circles that reached for a set of power cables. The Malden Township circle (right) was almost totemistic, whilst the formation at Teton, Idaho, was based on the classic Celtic cross patterns we are familiar with in the UK.

Many of these patterns are similar to those which occurred in the early days of the phenomenon in the UK. However, it is interesting to note that the crop circles happily appear in diverse crops, such as soya beans and maize, which are more widely grown in the USA and Canada.

(ABOVE) *Locust Grove, Serpent Mount, Ohio, USA. August 2003. Soya bean crop, approximately 150 feet*

(ABOVE) *Clyman, Wisconsin, USA. July 2003. Wheat crop, approximately 350 feet*

(ABOVE) *East Garafraxa, Ontario, Canada. August 2002. Wheat crop, approximately 80 feet*

(LEFT) *West Union, Ohio, USA. October 2003. Soya bean crop, approximately 150 feet*

(ABOVE) Malden Township, Ontario, Canada. July 1994. Wheat crop, approximately 200 feet

(LEFT) Teton, Idaho, USA. August 2002. Wheat crop, approximately 250 feet

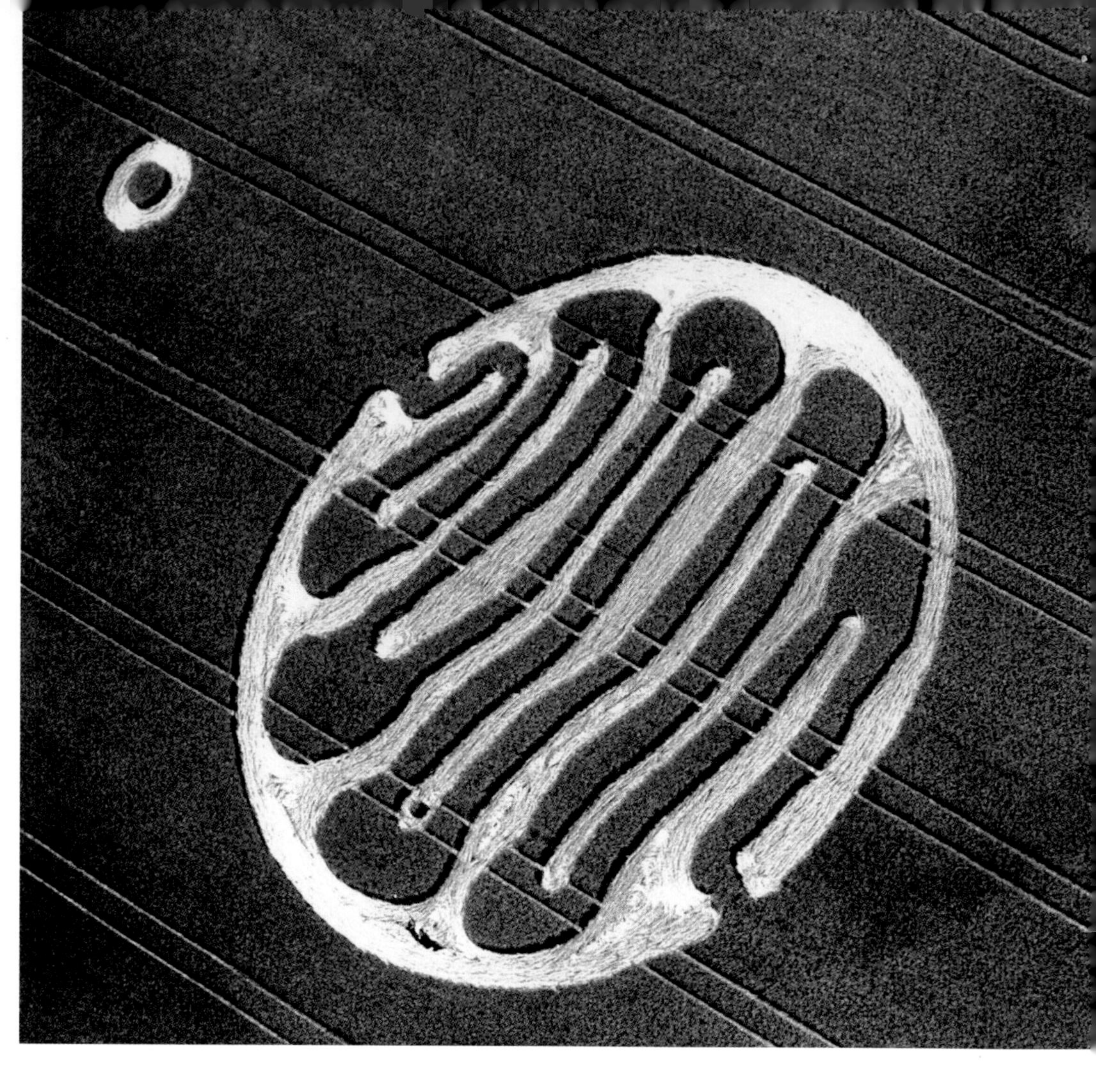

GERMANY AND SWITZERLAND

These two formations have a distinct European flavour. The first, at Ehlen, is a beautiful spiral in which the line seems serrated.

In contrast, the formation at Grombach is like oil on water. The wavy, meandering line is almost labyrinthine.

The circle at Desenberg (bottom right) is based on 'curves of pursuit', something we have seen in England.

At Thalheim, simple circular geometry created a criss-cross pattern around an inner circle.

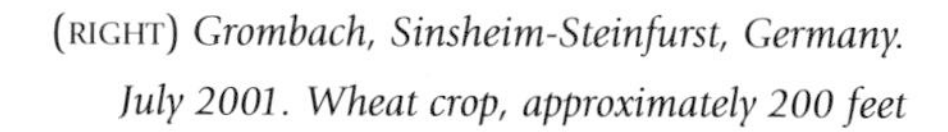

(RIGHT) *Grombach, Sinsheim-Steinfurst, Germany. July 2001. Wheat crop, approximately 200 feet*

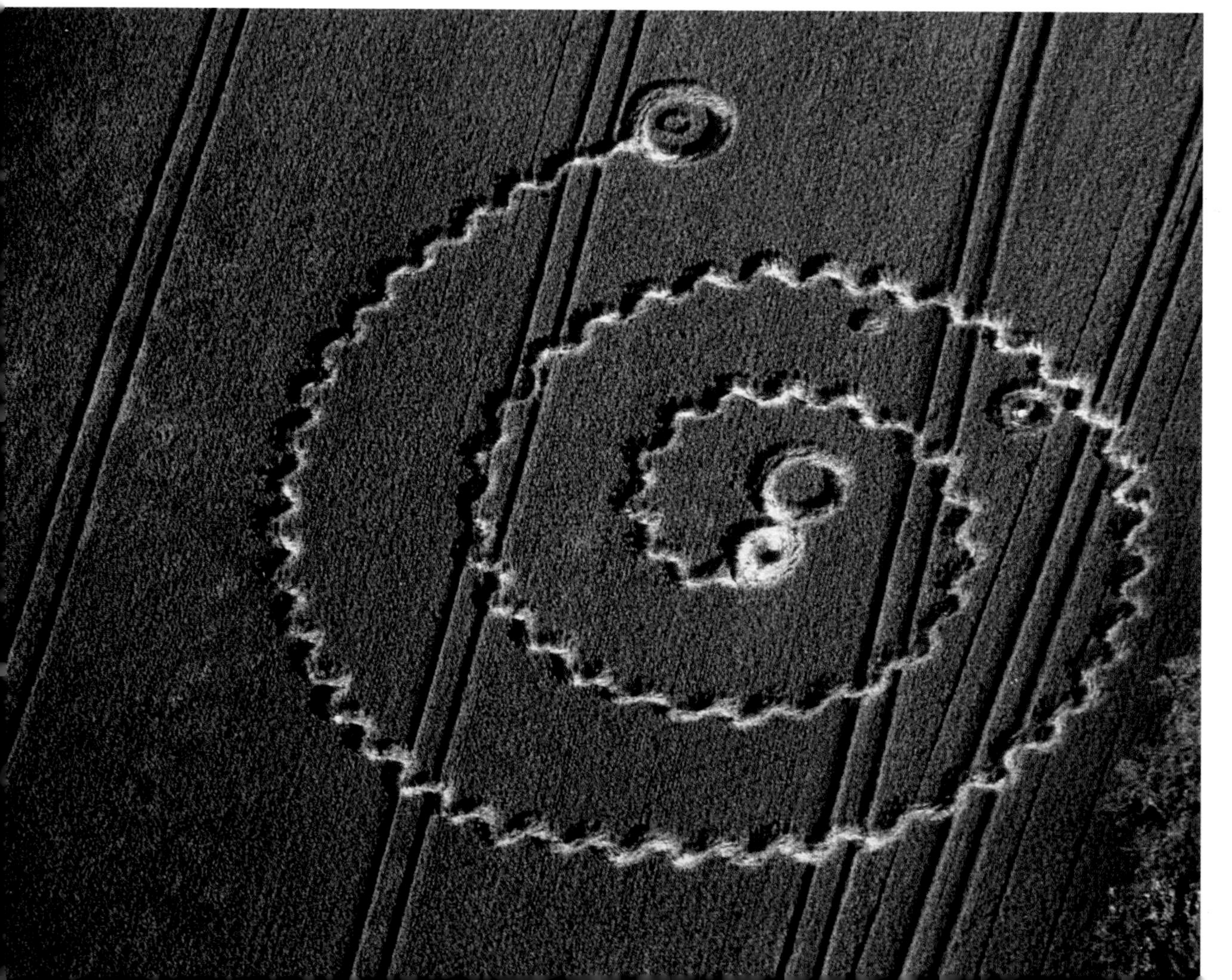

(LEFT) *Ehlen, near Kassel, Hessen, Germany. June 1999. Rye crop, approximately 120 feet*

Thalhiem, near Zurich, Switzerland. July 2004. Wheat crop, approximately 150 feet

(RIGHT AND BELOW) *Desenberg, Germany. August 2001. Wheat crop, approximately 150 feet*

SWEDEN AND THE NETHERLANDS

There have been a number of ice circles reported over the years. Researchers remain divided over whether these circles are a natural phenomenon or if they might be related to the crop circles. The ice seems to melt in a perfectly symmetrical fashion, leaving a ring of water exposed. Ice circles are very beautiful and ethereal and there have been several in Europe and the US.

The circle at Ketelhaven, in the Netherlands (bottom right), would not appear out of place in the English countryside; the circles at Valkenburg and Vlijem Noord are simpler designs. It is a six-fold spinner with ribbon-like arms. The circle at Valkenburg was a curving thought-bubble set, whilst the formation at Vlijim Noord was classic pictogram design – a type often seen in the early 1990s in the UK.

(ABOVE) *Piteälven, near Älsbyn, Sweden. January 1987. Ice, approximately 165 feet*

Vlijem Noord, Brabant, Netherlands. July 2004. Wheat crop, approximately 150 feet

(ABOVE) *Valkenburg, Limburg, Netherlands. June 2004. Wheat crop, approximately 120 feet*

Ketelhaven Flevoland, Netherlands. July 2003. Wheat crop, approximately 100 feet

CHAPTER ELEVEN

SIGNS AND WONDERS

... OF THE MODERN AGE

As is customary, we have saved the best for last – those crop circles that have the ability to awe, astonish and push the very limits of perception and belief. Their immediate visual impact is hard to ignore; even if we should quickly turn cynic, just for one brief moment we have been caught allowing ourselves to wonder. People often say that cynicism is born of a broken heart, perhaps in the case of the circles this is true. How many of us would truly love them to be the proof that we are not alone? Or confirm that we are in touch with something other than ourselves – a culture that might have wonderful things to teach us, wonderful stories to exchange. Perhaps we shouldn't be so dismissive of these forbidden yearnings or so harsh on ourselves. Perhaps mankind is lonely. After all, he appears to have no one with whom to compare himself, no other intelligent species with whom he can converse and share his wisdom, hopes, dreams, troubles and fears.

The crop circles, however, do seem to speak a universal language; a universal philosophy grounded in the archetypes that define our consciousness and the whole of reality. The circles might then be accepted as a step towards understanding and grasping that which could, one day, allow us to enter into a meaningful conversation with others, about matters beyond our own self-concern. More of this at the end of the book. But for now, prepare yourself to be astonished and maybe, just maybe, give yourself permission to dream a little.

(RIGHT AND OVER PAGE) *Milk Hill, Wiltshire, England. August 2001. Wheat crop, approximately 900 feet*

MILK HILL GALAXY, 2001

The Milk Hill Galaxy spiral should go down in history as the most astonishing crop circle of all time – so far. It appeared fully formed and perfectly constructed as the sun cast it first light over the hills of the Pewsey Vale in Wiltshire. It had been a filthy August night, wet and windy, the result of humid summer air meeting a colder weather front.

The extent of this crop circle simply beggared belief. It was unfathomable at

ground level, and it was possible to stand in the formation and not be able to see its end. One researcher described it as a giant confetti storm – a flurry of circles of all sizes, swept around whirlwind-like to create this beautiful design. Numbers came into play; most significantly, this formation iterated the number thirteen. There were thirteen circles in each of the six arms and also in the total number of circles – 409 (4 + 0 + 9 = 13). This seemed a very portentous event that spoke of change and transformation.

Eerily, just weeks later, the world was transformed by the 11 September attacks in New York. It's extremely doubtful that the crop circles predicted this event, but perhaps there was a just a flicker of something looming in the global unconscious, which was given expression by the appearance of this design.

This said, many found this circle an inspiration and a sign of the highest order that the world was infinitely more complex than they had ever imagined.

(BELOW AND RIGHT) *Milk Hill, Wiltshire, England. August 2001. Wheat crop, approximately 900 feet*

PICKED HILL, 2000

The beautiful Picked Hill formation was immediately reminiscent of the pattern found at the centre of a sunflower. The central pattern of the sunflower is generated by the Golden Section spiral, although that was not the case with this formation. The design derived from two sets of twenty-two spirals, one clockwise, and the other anticlockwise – giving a total of forty-four spirals. In addition, the crossing spirals created fourteen concentric rings. Forty-four over fourteen reduces to twenty-two over seven; we are more familiar with this fraction expressed as the decimal 3.142 or 'pi' (π), the formulaic number used to calculate the circumference of a circle.

NORTH DOWN, 2003

This wonderfully intricate design contained eleven concentric standing rings, into which had been pressed or swirled a myriad of tiny hoops or ringed circles. However, perhaps of more interest was its placement on the landscape. Originally, there were five round barrows (tumuli) in this field. Old maps mark the position of the fifth but it was destroyed at some point, and this circle appeared to restore the line of five, just for a few short months. Round barrows are something of a mystery in themselves. Not all were used for burial purposes and so the significance of the empty barrows is unknown.

(RIGHT) *North Down, Wiltshire, England. July 2003. Barley crop, approximately 350 feet*

Picked Hill, Alton Barnes, Wiltshire, England. August 2000. Wheat crop, approximately 250 feet

Avebury Trusloe, Wiltshire, England. July 2000.
Wheat crop, approximately 300 feet

AVEBURY TRUSLOE, 2000

This magnificent formation was undoubtedly associated with magnetic fields. The pattern recalls the magnetic field revealed by the way iron filings line up around a bar magnet. This is another example of how the crop circles seem concerned with making visible the invisible forces and principles that underlie our reality. Geometrically speaking, a form of rotational symmetry seems to be at work, originating from the two flattened areas close to the centre of the formation. This kind of patterning is created by continually repeating a curve or line whilst simultaneously and sequentially moving around in a circle. It is yet another expression of the spinning and circular element so venerated by the circle-makers.

GREAT SHELFORD, 2001

The Shelford Angel was a joyful, radiant image. With arms and wings extended, the delicate folds of her gown were beautifully realized. The tiny dark spots within the formation were birds on the ground; it seems apt that she should be accompanied by feathered companions.

The effect of this image on many of those who saw her was profound. They found her deeply moving. Angels are divine messengers, figures of hope, love, grace and deliverance.

Great Shelford, Cambridge, England. July 2001. Wheat crop, approximately 180 feet

CHILBOLTON RADIO TELESCOPE, 2001

The late summer of 2001 gave us two of the most unusual and controversial crop circles yet. In a field beside the Chilbolton Radio Telescope in Hampshire, two crop formations appeared that broke the mould in such a startling way that it was difficult at first to equate them with what had become the accepted nature of the crop circle phenomenon.

The first occurred on 14 August. It was a face inscribed into the crop using a dot-matrix methodology. What met the visitor upon entering the formation was a criss-cross of standing circles of varying sizes in every direction. Like Milk Hill, the ground experience proved fairly incomprehensible, but what was familiar was the beautifully swept and swirled crop. The second formation appeared six days later. It was even more bizarre – an oblong area containing a series of patterns and boxes. It was not long before it was recognized as a representation of the binary code first beamed into space from the Arecibo Telescope on Puerto Rico in 1974; however there were a few modifications. The 'message' apparently indicated that its creators were silicon-based and smaller than ourselves; they also indicated that they inhabited a binary star system. What are we to make of this and exactly whose is the enigmatic face?

(ABOVE) *Chilbolton Radio Telescope, Hampshire, England. August 2001. Wheat crop, approximately 150 feet*

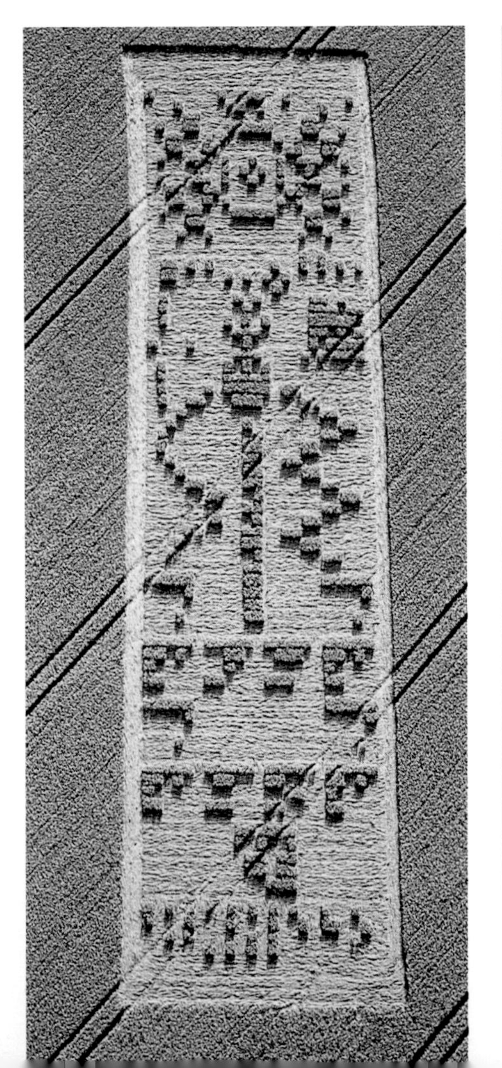

(LEFT) *Chilbolton Radio Telescope, Hampshire, England. August 2001. Wheat crop, approximately 250 feet*

(ABOVE AND FAR RIGHT) *Sparsholt, Hampshire, England. August 2002. Wheat crop, approximately 400 feet*

SPARSHOLT, 2002

This astonishing alien face and disc arrived in a Hampshire field, next to an array of radio masts, in a mirroring – of sorts – of the Chilbolton formations. If we had been struggling beforehand to grasp the archetypal, ambient geometric forms and number play of the crop circle phenomenon, then these two events seemed totally at odds with what we had understood so far. The disc was found to contain a form of binary code. It was a short message (a decoding appears above far right) that alluded to the hatred of deception and offered hope for mankind before abruptly ending. It was, in short, utterly bewildering. You might ask if these two formations are any part of the same phenomenon that we have been discussing. Opinion is divided. Either they constitute a profound communication or they are not what they appear to be. However, I do have to say that I have found the various reactions to this alien face extremely interesting; perhaps there is something to be learned for each and every one of us in examining our reactions to this highly provocative image.

(LEFT) *A decoding of the disc attached to the Sparsholt formation reads as follows:*

BEWARE THE BEARERS OF FALSE GIFTS
AND THEIR BROKEN PROMISES
MUCH PAIN
BUT STILL TIME
BELIEVE
THERE IS GOOD OUT THERE
WE OPPOSE DECEPTION

NORTH DOWN, 2003

The North Down formation was predictably christened The Molecule. This gigantic arrangement of circles (or discs) was the final event of the 2003 season. There are a total of seventy-eight circles, arranged in a loosely hexagonal fashion. The meaning of this design remains unclear and open to interpretation.

North Down, Wiltshire, England. August 2003. Wheat crop, approximately 450 feet

East Field, Alton Barnes, 2004

This strange and enigmatic design seems like some kind of device or apparatus. Once again, the meaning of such an image is inscrutable. It was nicknamed the 'Tesla' formation after the unconventional inventor Nicolas Tesla.

Alton Barnes, Wiltshire, England. June 2004. Wheat crop, approximately 600 feet

CROOKED SOLEY, 2002

One of the most beautiful and transcendent crop circles of all time, the Crooked Soley formation contained a harmony and synergy of sacred geometry and number that was simply inspired.

The picture you see here is one of a mere handful that exists of this circle. It was discovered by a pilot the morning it appeared, who alerted us to its presence. Since it was already August and the summer had been hot, we knew that it would not be long before the harvest, so time was of the essence and a flight was arranged.

As our helicopter approached Crooked Soley, the machinery was already in the field with the farmer trying to wave away the aircraft, making it clear that he did not want the formation to be seen. It was just a matter of hours before the circle had been chewed up by his harvester; our pictures are now the only record of this event, no other photographer was able to reach the location in time.

The Crooked Soley formation contained a perpetual DNA helix and also included a squared-circle proportion. That man (or the human being) is himself a meeting point of Heaven and Earth seems to be implicitly at the heart of this design.

Crooked Soley, Berkshire, England. August 2002. Wheat crop, approximately 350 feet

Silbury Hill, Wiltshire, England. August 2004. Wheat crop, approximately 350 feet

SILBURY HILL, 2004

This impressive formation mixed together iconic design elements from ancient cultures such as Egyptian, Mayan and even Greek. There is something utterly compelling about this image; the beauty of the inner feathered wing-like section is breathtaking. This crop circle seemed to speak of important wisdoms and ancient knowledge, yet it was quite impossible to convert that conviction into words.

Wayland's Smithy, Oxford. August 2005. Wheat crop, approximately 300 feet

WAYLAND'S SMITHY, 2005

The Silbury Hill circle had been the culmination of the 2004 season but it was also an exciting forerunner of the best designs of the 2005 season.

This beautiful formation appeared close to Wayland's Smithy, a covered long barrow (burial chamber) in Oxfordshire, and was greeted with awe and excitement. It was celebrated for its similarity to designs found in parts of the Ancient Mayan calendar.

Twenty box-like structures form the perimeter of the pattern itself. Travelling towards the centre, a series of standing rectangles seem to indicate some kind of coded information.

However, this amazing formation was just the penultimate circle of the 2005 season – there was more to come.

Woolstone Hill, Oxfordshire, England. August 2005. Wheat crop, approximately 450 feet

WOOLSTONE HILL, 2005

The superlatives begin to wear a little thin at this point. The circle at Woolstone Hill, close to the ancient chalk horse at Uffington on the Berkshire Downs, was definitely of the 'Signs and Wonders' variety. The size and complexity of design was simply astonishing. What made this formation so interesting was the fact that it contained a whole gallery of design elements, which had first been seen in various formations throughout that summer. Looking at a collection of images from 2005, one could see how this circle was an iteration and culmination of a series of themes that had been worked through that year. To walk in this crop circle was an unforgettable experience. The architectural space was simply phenomenal and many people commented on the uplifting feeling they experienced whilst inside.

Woolstone Hill, Oxfordshire, England. August 2005. Wheat crop, approximately 450 feet

WHAT NEXT?

The beauty of the crop circles lies not just in their awe-inspiring designs and spaces, but also in their continual evolution of form with each passing year. The exciting thing is that we never know where the circles will lead us next. The annual chase across the fields to experience and record these magnificent and curious happenings is as exhilarating as it is exhausting. And with each new formation there is something fresh to contemplate and discuss. Perhaps the real wonder of the crop circles is the way the principles and ideas they embody have the ability to change deeply the way people perceive the world. They constitute a remarkable challenge to our fundamental view of what reality really is.

CHAPTER TWELVE

'EN-SOULING' THE WORLD

ENDINGS

The crop circles present us with a view of the world that is rich with meaning and metaphor; they make visible the very designs of matter and life. The spaces they create are an invitation to come and take part in an exploration of these universal structures; to recognize the connection of all things in the patterned fabric of creation. They also seem to suggest that these shapes and patterns are an intimate part of our own thought processes; and that they are an archetypal structure upon which not only matter and life are based, but also lie at the heart of the structure of consciousness itself.

That sense of familiarity the circles sometimes evoke – that uncanny feeling that you know what these shapes are and what they mean, and that they are somehow vitally important – make so much more sense when looked at from this viewpoint.

The circles seem concerned with rebalancing our world-view and our sense of reality. In their own way, they are raising awareness of the fact that there is meaning as well as function behind creation, and that life and everything concerned with it has an innate purpose. No matter how you feel that the crop circles may have originated, they are bringing a richness and depth of inspiration to the fore. They 'en-soul' our world and breathe life and colour into the scientific machinery currently used to describe our universe. The circles seem to engender a view that such machinery is but the skeleton or bare bones of the universe, and that what we now need to understand is the flesh, the life-blood and heart of the wonderful creation around us.

Is there more to this reality than we can currently see? A cursory glance over the rich legacy of legend and myth held by our world's many cultures suggests that there is far more to our reality than we currently acknowledge in our minds and hearts. The crop circles are our 'signs and wonders', our symbols and guides, our dreams and aspirations made manifest in the fields. They are a counterbalance to the mechanical and functional reality that the western world promulgates. They are mandalas of healing that have spread across the face of the earth; they are an unconscious expression of our need to re-order and reconsider. In our turbulent times, the human race is faced with many choices and many dilemmas, and is being asked to re-evaluate its attitudes towards numerous issues, especially war and the environment. Perhaps the crop circles are an outward sign that this process is firmly under way. Throughout this book we have looked at a whole gamut of components which may be behind the crop circles. We have looked at earth energies, pizo-electrical effects, magnetic effects and the link between vibration and the formation of shape. We have looked at the astonishing use of number symbolism encoded in the circles and what some of that might mean. There are many possibilities for the origins of the circles: earth spirits, extra-terrestrials, extra-dimensional intelligences, Gaia (the consciousness of the earth itself) or, of course, large-scale international hoaxing.

Whoever the circle-makers are it is clear they prefer anonymity; it seems to me that they wish to be known by the quality of the fruits of their labour; the crop circles themselves. To be only interested in their identity, or the method by which they are make crop circles seems some how crude in comparison with the elegant and thoughtful works of art they put before us. The crop circles have resisted every attempt made to pin them down or explain them away, and after over fifteen years of being close to this phenomenon I have come respect that. There will always be people who are more interested in probing the circles scientifically, or those who want to spend their time with them building a case to prove or disprove the hoax theory. I am, however, content to sit, watch the the crop circles unfold and pay careful attention. The circles invite us on a journey of mutual exploration; I have the sense that neither side knows where it will end, but that the whole point of our interfacing is ultimately about the quality of the interaction.

We began this book by searching for a state of focused openness, one in which we suspended our world-view in the hope of gaining a better understanding of the beautiful crop circles. I suggest that rather than giving up and grasping for any explanation of this amazing phenomenon, we strive to maintain our openness, and approach the circles with the patient attentiveness that their works of art so gracefully demand.

Even if the mystery of the crop circles is never answered conclusively, they will leave an enduring impact on those who took the time to observe them. They will have changed forever their view of life and reality. And for those who may come long after the circles have disappeared, these pictures will serve as a snapshot of these difficult but hope-filled times.

Barbury Castle, Wiltshire, England. July 1991. Wheat crop, approximately 250 feet

ACKNOWLEDGEMENTS

Michael Glickman
Bertold Zugelder
Rob Luckins
Allan Brown
Kayleigh Douglas-Alexander
Alison Tredwell
Jeff Wilson
Frank Laumen
Peter Boerman
Eve-Marie Brekkestø
Werner Anderhub
Nancy Talbot
Ilyes
Karen Smith
Tharee Davis
Bryon Parker
Clas Svahn
Peter Stalder
Jeff Volk
Jan Dupont
All at Fast Helicopters, Andover, UK
Peter Vellacott
Josh Buxton
and finally, the circle-makers

PICTURE CREDITS

Page 84: Sound images from *Cymatics: A Study of Wave Phenomena and Vibration* by Hans Jenny © MACROmedia Publishing, 219 Grant Road, Newmarket NH 03857 USA. Used by permission. www.cymaticsource.com

Diagrams by: Bertold Zugelder, pages 18, 21, 24, 32, 40, 46, 54, 55, 60, 68, 72, 76; Michael Glickman, pages 45; and Allan Brown, page 82

Page 145: David Parker/Science Photo Library
Page 160-161: Courtesy of Tharee Davis
Page 162 (top, middle left and bottom left): Courtesy of Jeff Wilson
Page 162 (middle right): Courtesy of Karen Smith
Page 163 (top): Courtesy of the Windsor Star, Ontario
Page 163 (bottom): Courtesy of Bryon Parker
Page 164 (top and bottom): Courtesy of Frank Laumen
Page 165 (top): Courtesy of Peter Stalder
Page 165 (middle and bottom): Courtesy of Frank Laumen
Page 166 (top): Courtesy of Clas Svahn
Page 166 (bottom): Courtesy of Robert Boerman
Page 167 (top and bottom): Courtesy of Robert Boerman
Page 189: Courtesy of Richard Wintle

RESOURCES

CROP CIRCLE RESOURCES ON THE WORLD WIDE WEB

The crop circle phenomenon is chiefly reported on the internet. Many websites all over the world regularly post reports, pictures and information about the latest circles. Many also hold archival information.

www.temporarytemples.co.uk
Authors' website. Our website provides constant updates of the new circles throughout the summer months, and includes a comprehensive Image Library, details of our *Crop Circle Year Book* series, details of our Annual Conference, the films *65 Days* and *360°* and online shop.

www.cropcircleconnector.com
Leading UK and international crop circle reporting website, updates the new circles throughout the UK and abroad – largest crop circle website on the web.

www.ukcropcircles.co.uk
UK crop circle reporting site, excellent coverage of the interiors of the crop circles and on-the-spot field reports.

www.cropcircle-archive.com
Home of the crop circle archivist Bertold Zugelder. Bertold is a professional graphic designer who has been working with the crop circles for many years and provided most of the diagrams in this book. Recently he has produced a printed and bound archive of crop circle designs, containing over 5200 entries, each with diagram, date location and crop type. A must-have for any serious researcher or enthusiast. The archive is fully updateable and is available via his website. We highly recommend his important piece of work.

www.michaelglickman.net
Home of crop circle researcher and geometer Michael Glickman. Michael has written for crop circle periodicals and websites consistently since 1991 and his columns have produced delight and rage in equal measure. He believes that the Crop Circle phenomenon, operating entirely within the realms of form, geometry and number offers us profound, though veiled,information.

www.roundhillpress.com and **www.darroch.dircon.co.uk**
Websites of researcher and geometer Allan Brown. Allan Brown is an artist and geometer who has actively studied the crop circle phenomenon since 1996. Allan writes widely on the crop circles, sacred geometry and the metaphysical traditions that utilize number and proportion as means of spiritual integration and study.

www.bltresearch.com
The BLT Research Team's primary focus is crop circle research – the discovery, scientific documentation and evaluation of physical changes

induced in plants, soils and other materials at crop circle sites by the energy (or energy system) responsible for creating them and to determine, if possible, from these data the specific nature and source of these energies. BLT publishes these research results in peer-reviewed scientific journals and disseminates this information to the general public through mainstream articles and the internet.

www.invisiblecircle.org
Crop circle reporting website, useful for its reporting of European crop circles – particularly those from Germany.

www.uk.kornsirkler.org
Website of the Norwegian crop circle research group. Established in February 2000, collects and registers information about crop circles in Norway.

www.x-cosmos.it
Italian based website reports on all aspects of the paranormal including crop circles. Includes crop circles field reports, surveys and pictures.

www.dcccs.org
The Dutch Crop Circle Archive (DCCA) (Dutch Centre for Crop Circle Studies) reports and pictures of crop circles in the Netherlands.

www.circularsite.com
Another Dutch crop circle website run by Janet Ossebaard, crop circle author and researcher.

www.cropcirclenews.com
The Independent Crop Circle Researchers' Association (International) [ICCRA] Collective of crop circle researchers from the United States, which networks with researchers all over the US and beyond.

www.cccrn.ca
The Canadian Crop Circle Research Network (CCCRN) has been investigating the crop circle phenomenon in the prairies and across the country since 1995. Creating a unique liason with farmers and scientists, with volunteer research teams from coast to coast, it is the first and only research group of its kind in Canada.

www.cropcircleinfo.com
Colin Andrews is founder of Circles Phenomenon Research International, the first organization established specifically to investigate the crop circle phenomenon. Colin, with Pat Delgado, published the first major crop circle book *Circular Evidence* in 1989, which brought the phenomenon to the world's attention.

www.sacredbritain.com
Home of Glenn and Cameron Broughton, who lead tours to visit the UK crop circles from the US each year.

NON-CROP CIRCLE WEBSITES

www.welcometothedarkslide.co.uk
Rob Luckins has worked as principle editor on the crop circle films *65 Days* and *360°* in conjunction with Steve and Karen Alexander. He works closely with Steve and Karen on numerous crop circle projects and is a much sought-after portrait photographer.

www.lifeisround.com
Home of musician and philosopher Alexander Bell. Alex has provided the soundtrack for the films *65 Days* and *360°* by Steve Alexander, Karen Alexander and Rob Luckins. Alex also runs The Centre, in Northamptonshire, England.

www.fasthelicopters.com
Charter Helicopter Company based in Andover in the UK. Steve Alexander has worked with Fast Helicopters for many years; the vast majority of the photographs in this book were taken with the company. Fast Helicopters specialize in pleasure flights over the UK crop circles – highly recommended.

www.cymaticsource.com
The home of Hans Jenny's work into the science of sound and vibration – highly recommended.

SUGGESTED FURTHER READING

A Beginners Guide to Constructing the Universe by Michael S. Schneider. Harper Paperbacks, 1995
Crooked Soley by Allan Brown and John Michell. Roundhill Press, 2005
Crop Circles by Michael Glickman. Wooden Books, 2005
Cymatics by Hans Jenny. MACRO Media Publishing, 2001
Daimonic Reality by Patrick Harpur. Pine Winds Press, 2003
Sacred Geometry by Miranda Lundy. Wooden Books, 2001
Serpent in the Sky by John A West. Quest Books, 1993
Sun, Moon and Stonehenge by Robin Heath. Blue Stone Press, 1998
Supernatural by Graham Hancock. Century, 2005
The Colours of Infinity, Introduced by Sir Arthur C. Clarke. Clear Books

INDEX